The BOSS for 21st Century Organizations

Praise for *The BOSS for 21st Century Organizations*

"For leaders grappling with the tangible realities of integrating Artificial Intelligence and the principles of NeuroLeadership into their human resource strategies, this book offers a refreshingly practical roadmap. Drawing upon an impressive 40 years of hands-on experience, Dr. Mouriño bypasses abstract theoretical discussions to deliver concrete, actionable insights directly applicable to today's dynamic organizational and workforce challenges. You'll gain a clear and implementable understanding of crucial trends, the evolving expectations of your workforce, and proven strategies for fostering a synergistic relationship between AI-driven tools and indispensable human capabilities. Furthermore, the exploration of NeuroLeadership demystifies the science behind effective management, offering practical techniques to enhance team engagement, communication, and overall performance. This isn't just about understanding the future; it's about actively shaping it with practical, experience-backed guidance.

What truly sets this book apart is its commitment to immediate application and tangible growth. Beyond insightful analysis, it provides valuable, ready-to-use tools, most notably the included questionnaires designed for both individual and organizational assessment. These resources empower you to objectively evaluate your current leadership effectiveness and the "human intelligence" quotient of your workplace, pinpointing specific areas for development and improvement. If you're a forward-thinking leader determined to navigate the complexities of the AI-driven future with a grounded, human-centered approach and are seeking practical, experience-based solutions rather than just theoretical frameworks, this book will be an invaluable and immediately useful addition to your leadership toolkit."

—*David L. Gonzales*, **President and CEO of David L. Gonzales & Associates. and Board of Advisors and Senior Fellow of the Human Capital Center**

"Leaders must lead from a humanistic approach in today's world of constant chaos and disruption. Previous leadership books no longer address the challenges of today's business environment. Leaders must learn to be agile, deal with uncertainty, and encourage innovation while successfully creating an engaged workforce. This book provides valuable insight for leaders at all levels to develop a human-centric approach to leadership."

—*Dr. Nancy Zentis*, **CEO and Founder of the Institute of Organization Development**

"Aspiring, upcoming, and seasoned leaders will find in Dr. Mouriño's B.o.S.S. an evidence-filled rationale for leading today's and tomorrow's workforce. This book provides helpful guidance, tips, and resources for molding influential approaches to nurturing a high-performance environment. B.o.S.S. reveals a practical guide to avoid dysfunctional behaviors while delineating attitudes and actions to maximize human intelligence and potential."

—*Luis A. Marrero*, **MA, RODP, MMPP,**
Boston Institute for Meaningful Purpose, USA

"This book is more than just a guide—it's a mirror for anyone in a leadership role or aspiring to be one. It invites deep reflection on not just how you lead but why. What sets this book apart is its blunt honesty, practical wisdom, and clear insights. It does not romanticize leadership but shows it is earned, not granted. The author challenges the idea that a title alone makes someone competent.

The unique blend of personal stories, empirical research, and real-world observations makes the book relatable and credible. It also addresses why many young professionals shy away from managerial roles today. In a world increasingly dominated by Artificial Intelligence, it is easy to be seduced by efficiency and output. However, as the author rightly reminds us, AI cannot replace the human competencies that the workforce craves: empathy, vulnerability, presence, and authenticity.

As an academic leader, I find this book valuable for leadership development programs, executive education, and graduate-level management courses. I commend the author for offering such an insightful and challenging resource, urging us to rethink leadership as a position of power and a responsibility to guide, inspire, and impact other human beings."

—*Nubia Granja*, **PhD, Dean of Academic Affairs,**
Keiser University, Latin America Campus, USA

"In *The BOSS for 21st Century Organizations*, Edwin Mouriño provides concrete, powerful, and effective solutions to build people, teams, and relationships as never before. Every business, no matter the industry is ultimately the people business. It is how you grow and help others grow that will determine how far you will go! This is a MUST read for anyone in a supervisory, managerial, and leadership position. The number one reason why individuals leave organizations is unhappiness with their boss. Edwin Mouriño tackles that challenge by providing a clear game plan to put the human back in business leadership!"

—*Brian Biro*—**America's Breakthrough Speaker,**
husband, father, grandfather and author

"The BOSS for 21st Century Organizations is one of the best guides I've seen for anyone with human beings under their leadership. With his decades of experience as a coach, educator, and even an Air Force veteran, Dr. Mouriño-Ruiz really nails this one right on the head! Basically, he's saying it's time to move beyond just being a "boss" and really step into being a "LEADER." He emphasizes that in today's world, especially with all this AI around, human skills like empathy and good listening are more crucial than ever.

What you will find in this book

  i. What's happening in organizations now and how the workforce is changing – people want more than just a paycheck these days.
  ii. Why being human is so important even with all the cool AI tech.
  iii. How understanding our brains (NeuroLeadership) can make us better leaders by creating safe and clear environments.
  iv. Giving you practical things to think about to become a more effective leader and create a better workplace for your team.

He even throws in real-life "Reflections" from the workplace and some questionnaires to help you see how you and your organization are doing. At the end of the day this book is all about helping you on your own "reflective journey" to become a leader who really understands and connects with their team, making for a more human and successful workplace - The way it should be!"

—*Efrain "Ricky" Baez Jr.*, **MHR, SPHR, Chief HR Consultant**

"Edwin Mouriño-Ruiz, Ph.D., has written a book created by what I have personally seen him excel at doing as a colleague. That is to collect, assimilate, and align multiple sources of information and research, and apply it to management and leadership development. The result is an exceptional description of the emerging and continuing trends in the workplace. He covers topics ranging from artificial intelligence to neuroscience, with a specific focus on their application and integration with interpersonal skills development—what he has appropriately coined as "Human Intelligence". He shows new, as well as experienced leaders, what they need to know to create a healthy work environment in today's organizations. His focus on the need for leaders to know how to effectively build relationships is particularly important, and he sounds the alarm for those organizations that shortchange, or worse, ignore, this growing leadership imperative. A must read for every leader wanting to stay on the cutting edge of leadership and management in a fast-paced world that continues to accelerate."

—*Steve Swavely*, **PhD, CCP, Leadership Neuropsychologist**
and Author, Evolution Leadership Coaching, LLC

"Congratulations to Dr. Mouriño-Ruiz, on his timely and in-depth book. He has done a masterful job of addressing a very serious economic/human matter now into Pandemic+6 years. COVID+ 6 years is the evolution a new world order, which requires engagement and transparency between governments, organizations and people worldwide. We have learned that isolation from other nations and cultures, reduces our own worth as individuals and communities."

—*Luis G. Lobo*, **Executive Vice President, Retired**,
Truist Financial Corporation, USA

"In *The BOSS for 21st Century Organizations* Edwin Mouriño-Ruiz, Ph.D., presents a reflective and practical exploration of leadership in the contemporary workplace. Drawing from decades of experience as a leadership educator and practitioner, Dr. Mouriño discusses critical themes such as leadership development, the evolving nature of organizations, workforce psychology, human-centered management, and the integration of Artificial Intelligence (AI) with Human Intelligence (HI). His purpose is clear: to offer supervisors, managers, and executives actionable insights and tools for becoming more effective, compassionate, and adaptive leaders. This commentary analyzes the book's contribution to leadership studies and examines its practical relevance for today's organizations.

At the core of Dr. Mouriño's book is the concept of the "Smart Supervisor," a leader who balances technical competence with human-centered behaviors. He critiques the widespread practice of promoting high-performing individuals into management without adequate leadership training, arguing that technical excellence does not automatically translate into leadership effectiveness. Instead, Dr. Mouriño proposes a holistic leadership framework that emphasizes emotional intelligence, psychological safety, and human intelligence as essential to managing today's diverse and dynamic workforce. Key leadership frameworks explored include Leader-Member Exchange (LMX) Theory, emphasizing trust and relationship quality between leaders and subordinates; Servant Leadership, prioritizing empathy, humility, and service to employees; Neuro-Leadership, applying neuroscience insights to leadership practices, especially around empathy, stress management, and emotional contagion; and Human-Centered Organizations, which focus on dignity, respect, belonging, and engagement rather than mere productivity. A unique perspective Dr. Mouriño introduces is the urgent blending of Artificial Intelligence (AI) with Human Intelligence (HI). He warns that while AI will reshape workplaces, human empathy, compassion, and ethical decision-making will remain irreplaceable core competencies. Practically, these concepts are intended to be implemented through self-assessments, reflection questions, leadership behavior evaluations, and creating psychologically safe work environments. He also urges leaders to move beyond technical execution toward fostering meaning, autonomy, mastery, and purpose among their teams.

One of the book's strongest aspects is its deep practical relevance. Dr. Mouriño expertly bridges academic theories with real-world leadership challenges through case studies, reflections from the workplace, and practical tools like the Human Intelligent (HI) Workplace Questionnaire. His personal anecdotes and professional experience give the text authenticity and relatability. The integration of neuroscience, generational workforce trends, and diversity considerations makes the book forward-looking, addressing the challenges of 21st-century leadership head-on. The author's writing is accessible without oversimplifying complex ideas, making it valuable both for seasoned executives and first-time supervisors. Furthermore, the call for introspection, asking leaders to constantly reflect on how they are perceived and how they impact their teams, offers a powerful tool for continuous leadership growth.

Overall, "*The BOSS for 21st Century Organization*" is a vital, thoughtful contribution to leadership studies. It successfully addresses contemporary leadership gaps and offers actionable guidance. This book is highly recommended for organizational leaders, HR professionals, leadership development practitioners, and students in business and leadership programs seeking to build more human-centered, future-ready organizations."

—*Vitus Dono*, **LMS & Digital Systems Integrations and Principal at St Vitus Technical Institute, Ghana.**

"This book challenged me to examine my current leadership habits and consider what's truly effective versus what's just familiar. I want to revisit this idea regularly to assess how I'm growing and where I need to stretch further. What specific actions or changes could I implement in my daily practice to embody this principle more fully?"

—*Gabriel Davila Angel*, **Vice President and Head of Regional Unit LATAM at HOERBIGER**

The BOSS for 21st Century Organizations

Behaviors of Smart Supervisors:

Thoughts, Reflections, Insights, and Recommendations for Those in Supervisory, Managerial, and Executive Roles

Edwin Mouriño-Ruiz
Human Intelligent Workplace, LLC, USA

emerald
PUBLISHING

United Kingdom – North America – Japan
India – Malaysia – China

Emerald Publishing Limited
Emerald Publishing, Floor 5, Northspring, 21-23 Wellington Street, Leeds LS1 4DL

First edition 2025

Cover photo: iStock

Reprints and permissions service
Contact: www.copyright.com

British Library Cataloguing in Publication Data
A catalogue record for this book is available from the British Library

ISBN: 978-1-80592-159-2 (Print hardback)
ISBN: 978-1-80592-161-5 (Print paperback)
978-1-80592-158-5 and 978-1-80592-160-8 (Ebook)

Typeset by TNQ Tech
Cover design by TNQ Tech

CONTENTS

The most successful organizations in the 21st century will be those that recognize the human element in their enterprise, and the new sources of competitive advantage this can create. (Hamel, as cited in Westover, 2025)

ABOUT THE AUTHOR

Edwin Mouriño-Ruiz is a human capital practitioner, educator, and Air Force veteran. He has been in the business of helping leaders and teams help themselves for over 30 years.

He began college wanting to be a doctor to help others. This would eventually change when he received his BA in Psychology while in the Air Force. With his degree he changed his career field and entered what is now known as diversity, equity, and inclusion (DEI). He is a graduate of one of the most extensive DEI schools in the country, the DOD Defense Equal Opportunity Management Institute (DEOMI) where he became a Social Actions professional.

Since leaving the Air Force he has worked in a variety of organizations, industries, and roles, including management positions. His primary role has been as a leadership development professional where he has trained thousands of leaders at all levels, from executives to front line managers. He has also served as an Executive Coach and human capital consultant. He has also been a college professor for both graduate and undergraduate business students.

His philosophy has been one of helping leaders and their teams help themselves. He has also practiced this philosophy as a college professor. As a former student once wrote, "Dr. Mouriño is one of the most compassionate, knowledgeable and motivated servant-leaders I have ever come across — not to mention the best professor I've had the pleasure of working with."

He is founder and president of Human Intelligent (HI) Workplace where his vision is one of helping organizations become more human centered by creating an HI workplace especially in the era of AI. He has a PhD in Human Resources Development where his dissertation was on leader-member exchange (LMX) or leader-employee relationships in a virtual and co-located environment, something very relevant during and after the pandemic.

He is also an author of several books including: The Perfect Human Capital Storm and Gringo-Latino, and co-editor of Leading Diversity in the 21st Century. He has written numerous articles in a variety of sources and spoken at a variety of conferences and forums on topics related to the changing trends, DEI, and leadership.

He enjoys reading, music, biking, exercising, traveling, football, and watching good movies. He lives with his wife Sira and their poodle Mateo in Orlando, FL.

FOREWORD

I absolutely loved this book. From the very first chapter, I found myself nodding, smiling, and pausing to reflect—all signs (for me) of a book that truly matters. Edwin Mouriño-Ruiz has written exactly the kind of book today's leaders need—thoughtful, practical, deeply human, and refreshingly real.

In a world where organizations are navigating unprecedented change, shifting employee expectations, and the complexities of remote and hybrid work, this book could not be more timely. Edwin brings wisdom born from decades of experience—along with a heart for people—to every page. This is a guidebook for any leader who wants to lead with both their head and their heart.

Practical Wisdom for Any Leader

One of the things I appreciate most about this book is Edwin's ability to bridge timeless leadership truths—empathy, trust, listening, and self-awareness—with the pressing demands of today's workplace. He names the hard things leaders face: managing uncertainty, leading diverse teams, and fostering human connection in a digital world. But he doesn't leave readers stuck there. This is not a book of quick fixes—it's a book of transformation. With reflective questions, actionable ideas, and practical tools, Edwin invites leaders to grow without guilt. His voice is that of a wise mentor—credible, compassionate, and committed to helping others lead with courage and authenticity.

For Any Leader Who Wants to Have a Legacy Impact

Whether you're a brand-new supervisor or a seasoned executive, this book offers a roadmap for your leadership journey. New leaders will find guidance to avoid common pitfalls and start strong. Experienced leaders will find a challenge to stay humble, curious, and people-centered. And for all of us somewhere in between, this book offers wisdom, encouragement, and practical next steps.

In a world hungry for more human-centered workplaces, Edwin has given us a true gift. This book calls us to reflect not just on what we do as leaders—but on how we show up, how we engage with our people, and ultimately, what kind of leadership legacy we want to leave. I'm grateful for Edwin's voice and know readers everywhere will be better leaders—and better humans—because of the specific ideas recommended in this book."

Dr. Beverly Kaye, Thought Leader, Speaker, Co-Author of *Love' Em or Lose 'Em: Getting Good People to Stay, Help Them Grow or Watch Them Go: Career Conversations Organizations Need* and *Employees Want, Up is Not the Only Way: Rethinking Career Mobility, and Hello Stay Interviews, Goodbye Talent Loss.*

ACKNOWLEDGMENTS

I want to thank the Lord, for helping me along this journey. I want to share my appreciation for the love and support of my life, my wife. For her patience and as the key person who serves as a mirror for me. As I've said behind every good man is a greater woman. Recently I was corrected, instead of "behind every good man" I should use "next to every good man" and I agree. To my grandparents, mother, and uncles, The Ruiz family who put their thumbprint in my life and provided me the opportunity to achieve what I have. May they rest in peace and look down upon me with a smile.

Last, to those few I've worked for that I consider where a good model of a boss for me. I've had many bosses over my work career, but few that I truly believed were effective bosses. To Shirley Jones, who made my time at Lockheed Martin a positive experience. To the Lt. Colonel (sorry forgot his name) who gave me a second chance when I needed it as a young, enlisted airman. To Larry Hogue, who told me once, we won't work together forever, but let's make it the best time we can while we do. And last, to Dr. Stephen Swavely, who listened, coached, demonstrated empathy, and became a friend over time. Thank you all, wherever you may be for being a great BoSS to me and a better human being, each of you.

CHAPTER 1

INTRODUCTION

In my time in the corporate setting, I've noticed the promotions of great individual contributors to management without the proper training. —Edwin Mourino

Tomorrow's Companies will need to have the brains of a Business School Graduate and the heart of a Social Worker. — Friedman (2005)

Toto, we're not in Kansas anymore. —Fleming (1939)

These above quotes capture the essence of the state of organizations and its leadership in more cases than not. Over the years too many organizations have promoted great and high productive individual contributors to the positions of management. The thinking has and unfortunately continues today, that if they are one of best workers, then it only makes sense that they'll be a great boss. This is further highlighted in a Fast Company article titled "85% of new people managers receive no formal training" (Chamorro & Carucci, 2024), imagine almost 9 out 10 of those in a leadership position with no formal training taking responsibility for the most valuable resource of an organization, its workforce.

And while this is as of this year, I noticed this trend many years ago (last century to be exact) when I transitioned from the Air Force to the civilian sector and noticed that there were more than should have been put into a supervisory capacity without some form of development. In the Air Force, you did not step into a supervisory position without attending some form of military leadership development.

We have also found when people are not skilled, trained, or competent in a particular aspect of their job, they get anxious which obviously raises stress.

The BOSS for 21st Century Organizations, pages 1–16
Copyright © 2026 by Emerald Publishing Limited
All rights of reproduction in any form reserved.
doi:10.1108/978-1-80592-158-520251010

Something that we will address later in this book but might also add as to why some of the younger segment of the workforce are not necessarily interested in stepping into a management role or why some already in it, would step down if they could.

While some might consider this more relevant to newly promoted first line supervisors, I'd recommend a reconsideration on this thought. I have unfortunately seen more than I care to consider, of ineffective mid-level managers and executives in leadership roles. They have obviously been successful in delivering on the results and objectives in front of them and in turn been promoted to higher level management and executive roles. But as I have heard and observed over the years, at what costs or "how many bodies have they left in the path" as they progress up the management chain? This might be one of the reasons that in their book, *The Mind of the Leader*, Hougaard and Carter found that 35% of workers would give up a pay raise to see their boss fired.

In addition to this, while I've been in the area of leadership development for almost four decades, I am still today hearing of, seeing, reading, and finding research that highlights the need for better leaders. And anyone reading this book that is in a leadership role, will attest as to how difficult the job can be sometimes. A recent article highlighted the three toxic habits by bosses that include public scoldings, perfectionism, and unnecessary arguments (Jackson, 2024). The author highlight findings by almost 50% of Human Resources that have experienced workplace violence, including harassment as recent as 2019.

The fact that we're still speaking, writing, and educating on ensuring that leaders don't do this, especially with the amount invested on leadership development, by some estimates over $60 billion, says a lot about the importance of this topic. It also begs the question, why? Why are we still here with so much invested on leadership development? What is missing? It is not just that new and younger individuals step into the roles. Because some of the issues I've highlighted so far and more to come later have been done by those that have been in management for some time.

When it comes to those in executive positions, it reminds me of a time when I was part of a team responsible for creating a mentoring program for high potentials. We went around the room and discussed which executives should be mentors. Those not selected were mainly because they were considered ineffective leaders and role models and as an executive would not be considered good mentors. Yet here they were, in an executive role with influence over so many. This says a lot about what was really important for some organizations.

The second quote is particularly important for present and future leaders. As Marshal Goldsmith titles one of his books, "What got you here, wont' get you there." This holds true for those promoted to a supervisory capacity at any level where the skills necessary for success are not technical, but human or interpersonal skills. As I've always asked participants in my sessions or in my coaching engagements, how do you believe you're doing as a leader? And I add to this question, what would others say that work with you or for you? This usually gives them pause unless they are completely oblivious to their behaviors and how others may be perceiving their actions.

The third quote gets to the point that times and expectations have changed from the workforce. The psychology of the workers with their expectations of today are different from the past or perhaps just more prominent. The pandemic I believe has created a global tipping point for what the workforce is expecting. Many are craving meaning and purpose in life, but few people are finding such fulfillment at work. Today's worker's expectations are rapidly changing. Unfortunately, most companies have not evolved to keep pace with all of these changes.

Numerous articles and books are continuing to be written about people looking for purpose, meaning, happiness, and a positive workplace experience. In a Ted Talk by Dan Pink, he goes on to point out with research that what motivates most of us at work is purpose—doing or being part of something bigger than us, mastery—ongoing development, irrespective of age or career stage, and autonomy—having our will over control and choice about how to do something, in other words, not being micromanaged.

"You are how you lead." We used this phrase when we educated leaders in a leadership development organization I worked for. By this we meant, and got further into that their journey, that early imprints in life by others and circumstances, could have an impact on their present leadership behaviors. An example that comes to mind is the perfectionistic leader. Where did they pick up this mindset and in turn make it part of their leadership philosophy and behaviors? How is it being perfectionistic impact the individual leader behavior and their workforce? It might be something else for you or something you've noticed in others in a leadership role. This is something worth reflecting on as you read this book.

And I know being in a leadership role is not easy. I've been there. I am always amused by how many in my undergraduate or in some graduate classes that are not in a management position have that as a goal. And as I've always mentioned, be careful what you wish for. Looking at the position from the outside might seem appealing due to role, salary, privileges, etc. But those that are reading this and have been or are in a leadership role know both the pros and cons of the position. Which is probably why there is an increase in the younger generation seeming to not want this role as much and more managers wishing they could get out of it.

A few questions to consider are, when you perform in your role of boss is how do you engage with your team? How do you treat them? How do you treat each of your team members? Will or do you have favorites and gain the resentment from some or will you be fair with everyone? Are you aware of any of your blind spots or biases? This is why I have written this book. This book is for experienced managers and executives, and for newly minted supervisors, managers, filled with insights of both good and not so good practices and behaviors by those in a managerial capacity. The book also includes tools, techniques, and approaches for those in a managerial capacity to consider. But more importantly, I've written this book to help you reflect along the way about how you might be performing in a leadership role?

I want to sincerely thank you for selecting this book. Since as of last check, there is an estimated 15,000 books and over 11 million hits on Google for the topic of leadership. My hope is that as you read through it, you reflect and consider what can I learn from this that I had not thought of before or truly, deeply considered and should consider going forward? Because information is not transformation. I do hope you find something new in reading this book, or at least to something to think of differently that will help you reflect on how to be a more effective leader or boss. As you read through this book, I hope you truly reflect and ask yourself how do you believe you are doing and more importantly how might others believe you are doing?

As you read this book, I will first outline who this book is for and why I've written it, especially with so many books written on the topic. Following this, I will highlight what trends are taking place and what the implications for organizations, their leadership team, and the workforce. Next, I will take you into the psychology of the 21st century workforce and what they are expecting into today's workplace from their organizations and leaders.

Next, I will highlight some additional issues impacting the workforce and their leaders. I will also address how technology, in particular Artificial Intelligence (AI) is and will impact organizations going forward and the implications for leaders and its workforce. I will also highlight how neuroscience and neuroleadership, a growing and important aspect of today's leadership information have implications for leaders. Last, I will take you into what you as the boss can do by reframing your approach more so from a leader's perspective.

Throughout this book I've included some quotes of former colleagues and students (some cited and some not-as they preferred) who have had good and bad experiences with effective and ineffective superiors titled "Reflections from the workplace." This is intended to provide some context and insights of experiences workers can have in their workplace depending on the behaviors of their superiors. There might be one good or bad one or more that seems familiar. As you read them, consider, have you experienced or observed something similar—especially if it is a potential negative experience? If it is positive, consider the same. But most importantly, honestly reflect on if anyone may have experienced any of these while working for you. Sort of a conscious gut check.

You will also have access to two questionnaires. The first one will help you assess and/or evaluate how human-centered and in particular human intelligent your workplace is. Second, you will also have a leadership questionnaire that you can use to evaluate your leadership behaviors and practices and also allow you to get 360 feedback from your staff, colleagues, and management if you so choose to use this way (which I recommend).

Both of these questionnaires are intended for reflection and other's perspective on how you see your organization based on being a human intelligent workplace, your leadership effectiveness, and organizational readiness for change. They are also intended for you to gain a wholistic picture, by having others in your organizations to complete them also. This way you can compare your perceptions with those that your leadership behaviors will have an impact on during their tenure with you. They are created to serve as a practical and personal (your point of view) as you perceive your organization when it comes to human intelligence (HI) (as I've defined it), your organization's readiness for change, and your leadership effectiveness. I hope and believe you will find them helpful as you reflect on your organization and yourself as a leader.

In summary, you will have an opportunity to learn, relearn, reflect, think through, and consider how can I implement what I might need to in order to continue to grow and increase in my effectiveness as a leader. You will gain insights from others on their experiences with effective and noneffective leaders. You will get an opportunity to see visuals that will hopefully provide you insights on what is needed going forward. Last, you will have three evaluation questionnaires to use either by yourself and/or with other's perspective (my recommendation to gain a better comprehensive view). I truly hope this books helps you help yourself as you reflect on being an effective leader.

Reflections from the workplace…

"I worked for someone who had the habit of 'passing the buck'. In other words, he blamed his subordinates for failing to achieve their targets, but never thought he was partly responsible for the problem."

Who Is This Book for?

This book is intended for those with extensive experience in a managerial or executive role, for those that have recently been tapped to step into this new role, and/or for anyone considering a supervisory role. Before we begin it is important to at least layout some basic definitions on the key terms used in this book. While there are hundreds of definitions for the following terms. Webster defines *boss* as one who directs or supervises workers.

Cambridge dictionary defines *management* as the activity or job of being in charge of a company, organization, or team of employees. And Mckinsey defines *leadership* as a set of behaviors used to help people align their collective direction, to execute strategic plans, and to continually renew an organization. Drucker, considered by some as the father of management has been credited with differentiating management and leadership in the following manner, "Management is doing things right; **leadership** is doing the right things." Add to this that is has been noted in different venues that you as someone in a managerial/executive role, you lead people and manage things.

Irrespective of your preferred definition, the important piece to take away from the above is that someone in a managerial capacity is responsible for directing and influencing others to accomplish organizational objectives and deliverables. That it is the yen and yang of those in a supervisory capacity. And that balancing these two is an imperative for your success and those working with you.

The other takeaway and consideration is that it is important to put the human back in managerial behaviors and practices and in organizations as those of you in leadership roles and your teams work to deliver on the strategic and organizational objectives. It is for this reason, that I will be focusing on in this book on the leadership side of the equation. Because I have noticed more than my share of those in leadership capacity trying to manage their workforce. I hope as you read through this book, you'll come to the conclusion (or maybe already realized it but had not thought about as much), that creating a human-centered organization is going to take more of a human touch and for you to tap into your HI. Because AI will not solve all of the people and workforce issues.

Over time many have been educated and/or informed to believe in charismatic individuals. Because we know and see them when they walk into a room. They stand out and call attention to themselves. But the research highlights that the better leaders are those that are humble versus charismatic (Chamorro-Premuzic, 2020). This sort of supports the servant-leadership model and theory. And while there are many models and theories on leadership, my goal with this book is that irrespective of the models or theories, you consider what are the proper leadership behaviors you need to demonstrate for today and tomorrow's workforce?

It has been noted that employees now expect their manager to care about them personally, but many leaders still don't know how to do it. And what it will take going forward is "empathy, curiosity, compassion, attention, and acceptance, which cannot be replaced by technology" (Posner & Whitehouse, 2023). Real estate, technology, and humans are an organization's most expensive resources. How you use them going forward will impact you and your organizational success. The focus for this book is on your human workforce and your interactions with them as a leader (for those in a present leadership role).

For those not in one, consider how you're being treated by your manager and what do you hope to do once you step into the role?

Something else to consider is the following. If you google "descriptions of my boss," you come across many hits one of them that highlights 10 must traits of great bosses. Some of them include trust, mentor, motivator, honesty, high emotional intelligence, willingness to learn, and compassion among others (Insperity Staff, 2023). The question you should consider asking yourself, would those that work for me or with me use these words to describe me? That is part of what I hope you'll reflect on as you read this book.

To the point of putting human back in organizations, a fairly new term that has begun to be written about is the human centered organization. In a paper by IBM (IBM Human Centered) human centered organizations have been described as **companies whose company culture puts the person at the center of their activity,** rather than focusing only on sales and productivity. They tend to focus on creating better human experiences and care about its diverse teams among others. In order for this to happen, those in managerial roles, or the bosses, will play a crucial role in creating great workplace environments by ensuring their workforce is supported and engaged.

All of these factors are important to consider with others to follow. But another key point to consider is that there is an increasing number of those in a leadership role that would welcome the opportunity to become an individual contributor again, if their pay was not affected. Because the stress that comes with being in a managerial role has been and continues to increase.

In addition to the above, there is a growing challenge for organizations. Increasingly, young workers are resisting the opportunity to become a manager. Some of the reasons highlighted by Mr. Wong in his article, "Young workers don't' want to become managers" are due to low trust in their managers, he found a mere 21% strongly agreed that they trust their managers. The second reason is the pressures that come with being in a managerial role and a decrease in maintaining some semblance of work-life balance (Wong, 2023).

Reflections from the workplace…

"I had a boss who was not a boss, but a leader. They valued and had empathy for the team while driving us toward success."

Executives

For those in Executive roles, VP and above this is for you as part of your continual learning, reflections, and development. Most effective executives I have worked over my career are in a constant learning mode. They bring their experiences to bear, but also realize the workplace is constantly changing, and if they want to remain relevant, they need to continue to learn, adapt, and evolve. On occasion I have run into some executives that seem to come across as they think they know it all, don't have much to learn and sometimes even somewhat arrogant. I'm sure as you read this, you think of someone that fits this category or might not believe or think this is you. More importantly is to assess, what do your direct reports think? Are you humble and vulnerable enough to check into this? Where are you and what would others say?

There has been quite a bit of research from a variety of perspectives as to what those in executive positions need to do be better bosses. In her article, "3 soft skills separate highly successful CEOs from most people-here's how to master them" (Jackson, 2023). The author points out that many CEOs are losing their sense of humanity. Which aligns with some of the research that highlights that as one gains power, they lose empathy, a critical skill and competency for today's leaders. She goes on to point out that the three skills are visibility-ensuring you're being seen by your workforce, particularly during organizational changes, vulnerability, which means highlighting your humanity, and last verbal which is about communicating and more importantly listening.

On a positive note, the fact that you're reading this book is a good sign that you want to continue learn, reflect, and improve. This is important, because as an executive, you have influence over many in your organization, on the overall direction of the organizational strategy, and an impact on the overall climate and culture of the organization.

Mid-Level Managers and Directors

For those at these levels of the organization, this book is for you as you continue to grow, develop, and learn while trying to manage both upward with your respective executives (and boss), and lead those in the organization below you, including your management team and their staffs. You're in the mid-level role trying to drive organizational strategy directed from the executive teams with the leaders reporting to you and their employees. You're responsible for trying to begin the process of making organizational strategy real through your functional areas of responsibility.

You're in the unique position of managing upward while managing your team, without making the mistake of being seen as someone that just manages upward and forgets his/her team that are helping you on the department, function deliverables. As you read this book consider an interesting article that made the point that the philosophy going forward should be that middle managers are the core of organization (Field et al., 2023). This books provides you an opportunity to reflect and consider where do you have to continue to improve. Where you can continue to grow as the boss and perhaps and hopefully continue to grow within the organization whether that be where you are or your next level.

Front Line Supervisor

As a front-line supervisor or newly minted supervisor this book will hope-fully provide you some things to consider as you learn your new role. You've obviously been successful in your individual contributor role, and because of this you've been promoted not to do the work, but to get it done through others. Now you get to learn and grow both your management skills and leadership capabilities. In this book, you get to gain insights into what it means to be the boss. How to work on minimizing the negative aspects that some in these positions bring to bear and how to demonstrate the effective qualities of positive boss behaviors.

If you are a newly promoted supervisor, it probably means that your management saw a good work ethic in you. It means that you are seen as someone that they could depend on and felt that you demonstrated the qualities to be a good leader for the department and organization. It means that your management saw someone that they felt could move the orga-nization forward in a positive way because you delivered in your role as a mechanic, engineer, accountant, nurse, teacher, janitor, security guard, nurse, doctor, or whatever role you have been in where you demonstrated success by achieving results. But if there is one message this book tries to convey, it is that what got you here is not necessarily what will help you be successful in your new role of a boss.

In the past I believed that executives made the biggest impact on their workforce. But I have been revisiting and rethinking this over the last few years. I believe you the front-line leader has a bigger impact on your work-force. After all, they see or interact with you on a daily basis and get to see you up close and personal.

If you are one of those individuals already in a supervisory, managerial, or executive role, you have experiences, both good, bad, and indifferent. You have habits you have formed as to how to lead your department or organization. And with this you bring your behaviors, insights, experiences, insecurities, political savviness, networking, and ways to create your respec-tive environments, department and/or organizational culture that affects those that work under your supervision.

Irrespective of your level and experience, you will impact those around you. There is the concept of known as Emotional Contagion, which basically means that your emotions are contagious and highlights that the emotions you demonstrate will affect those around you. If you're in a good mood, or under stress it will serve like a pebble that is dropped in a lake or pond, it will create ripples. Those ripples may be good or not. Depending on your behaviors, what you say and don't say.

This book looks to begin by highlighting the current trends impacting organizations and society in general. It looks to highlight what the current and future employee is expecting in an organization and what key role you play as the new boss. It looks to bring to the forefront some perspectives for you to consider as you transition to your new role or continue to grow in your leadership role. My hope is to help you reflect that the old "golden rule" treating others like you would like to be treated is not enough in today's workplace. That perhaps you might consider the "platinum rule" and treat others how they like to be treated.

The term the boss, similar to the term feedback has unfortunately been interpreted at times as something negative. They do not have to be, are not always, but they have at times. Regarding feedback, it is mainly because when someone hears that their management wants to provide them feedback, it is usually for some mistake or something they are not doing right. We have done this so much, that we seemed to have conditioned our workforce into fear, uncertainty, or uncomfortableness when the word is used. Our brain tends to interpret the word feedback with something negative.

So, there is an opportunity for those in the boss position, to begin to use this term for both good and developmental conversations. There is also an opportunity for those in the boss position to begin to model the behavior they expect. That by opening themselves up to feedback and requesting it from their teams so others can provide them feedback on what they may doing well and what to improve on as the boss, can lead to the feedback not be seen as only negative. Particularly when you the leader become vulnerable by being open to continual learning from others.

When it comes to the term boss it has just been used to represent someone in a management or supervisory capacity, irrespective of level in the organization, whether this individual is a first line, mid-level management, or in the executive ranks. If you look up the definition of boss in Webster, you find that it defines it as "a person who exercises control or authority." Much has been written about the boss. If you were to google "books on boss," you will get 12 million hits. Yet here we are. Much has been written, companies have invested millions on leadership development in order to help those in a managerial role and to develop their skills. Despite this, one study found that 35% of employees would pass up a pay raise to see their boss fired (Hougaard et al., 2018).

Reflections from the workplace…

"I worked for someone with very poor interpersonal skills and never thanked anyone for their accomplishments."—Mariano Estrada

---

There are probably a variety of reasons for this, but this same book goes on to highlight that one reason may be due to lack of listening when in another study they found that only 8% of leaders are effective communicators and listeners. One reason I believe this is the case is due to something David Rock from the NeuroLeadership Institute has highlighted and that is that organizations have hired and promoted generations of managers with robust analytical skills and poor social skills (2013). This unfortunately happens more than it should, and it does a disservice to those in these positions, to their staffs, and to the organizations.

What this tends to create is a situation where individuals step into this role not realizing what is really needed in their new role or have not been trained in the expectations for their new role as "the boss." In addition, for those with extensive management and executive experience, they have in some cases been rewarded or not held accountable for inappropriate behaviors and in some cases continue to be promoted up the chain. I say this as someone who has seen senior executives not demonstrating effective leadership behaviors yet achieve on their deliverables while leaving bodies along the way.

Fortunately, in spite of the above many have worked for someone that was a good boss. And I wish someday, books like this one will not be necessary. But up to now, I unfortunately see the need for some time to come. I hope as future, present, and experience leaders read this book, they take a good look in the mirror and truly reflect on how they can continue to improve. By ensuring those in leadership positions improve can lead to more humane organizations, engaged and overall healthier workforce.

So, if you're the new boss, welcome to your new role. If it is another promotion in your managerial or executive journey, congratulations. Some of you might be excited while others a little nervous or maybe both. We hope this book helps point you both in a better direction and enable you to be not only successful, but effective.

I am assuming and hoping that since you've picked up this book to read, you're hoping to gain some insights to help you in helping yourself in your new role. Something to consider, that irrespective of the position you're in from a managerial perspective, front line supervisor up through executive there is a mental shift that has to be made (Bryant, 2023) . It involves identifying and sharing your core values, setting the bar for your team, function, or organization, and enhancing your self awareness. In order to help and lead others, you'll need to lead and help yourself and one way to do this is by ensuring you have an increased awareness of yourself.

Reflections from the workplace…

"I worked for someone that understood how to lead individuals by bringing them together to accomplish a goal. They removed obstacles for the team, coached, supported, and delegated. They adapted their leadership style to the different stages of development that the individuals on the team were."—Eli Stephan

---

Something I have found interesting is the following. Before you stepped into your first managerial role (and for those considering it), you probably never realized that you would become a celebrity, a quasi/semi psychologist, sociologist, and anthropologist. So why do I say this?

I say celebrity, because as one in a managerial role, whether this is a first line supervisor, director, or VP, you are always under the spotlight. Your staff and those in the organization are watching every move, action, and what you say or don't say. I have over time thought the spotlight would be more on the executives, but I'm beginning to believe that it might be brighter on the first line supervisor or at a minimum on the direct manager of the subordinate because they have a direct impact on their staff on a daily basis. There is a concept known as Emotional Contagion, which basically means that your emotions (boss) are contagious. How you show up, if you're in a good mood or not, will have an impact on your staff. You can either be a pebble dropping in the water or a rock splashing.

I mentioned a quasi-psychologist. What I mean by this is that when you're dealing with someone on your team in a one on one, or just how you interact with them, there is psychology at play. Both of you are human and your personality strengths and insecurities can come into play when you are both interacting. How you show up as their superior will play an important role on your interactions. Do you consider them a good team member or not? Do they feel psychologically safe around you and trust you? Whatever is the answer to these questions and others will play a role into your psychological interfaces, some of them unconsciously (more about this later).

Regarding being a quasi-sociologist is all about the team dynamics and interfaces among the team and the environment you create for your team. Do you have favorite or those that you engage with more often than others, or your "go to" staff? While you may not, others may see this as you are having your favorites. The team dynamics from one department or group to another can be seen as possibly as different. This is how you behave as a leader, executive, or department manager and what type of environment you might create.

Regarding the quasi-anthropologist piece, as a boss you play a role in the type of climate or culture you create whether it be in your department or function. Anthropologists study cultures around the world. Some organizations have actually considered bringing in anthropologists into their organization to assess their organizational culture. Just like your organization has a culture, you within your area of responsibility, create your own departmental and/or functional culture.

An important note, to all psychologists, sociologists, and anthropologists I am in no way trying to minimize your role and profession, as they are very reputable professions and I once seriously considered two of these as my professional aspirations. However, I do hope you agree that those in a managerial capacity do play a particular role, while small in the areas that you call and consider as your profession. Which is another reason why they can always use your professional assistance, especially with the increased stress that some work environments and those in a leadership role can impose on others and on themselves.

Why This Book?

> Over a period of many years, leaders have consistently given low marks to the quality of leadership in their organizations…despite all of the effort and investment in leadership development—innovative new modalities, up-to-date content, business simulations, accelerations pools, 70/20/10 approaches, better diagnosis of strengths and areas of development—widespread improvement in leadership effectiveness remains elusive. Pfeffer (2015)

I have been conducting leadership development workshops for almost forty years. I have consulted and provided executive coaching to numerous managers and executives along the way on enabling them to be better at their role as the boss. I have also been a manager myself. I have seen first-hand what effective behaviors *are* and *are not.*

I began in the Air Force and have continued afterward in the civilian sector in a variety of industries. Along the way I've come across some interesting experiences with both effective and ineffective supervisors (aka the boss). One thing I found the military did well before promoting someone to a supervisory role was to send them off to some form of leadership development workshop. Regardless of level, as you continued to grow in your rank, there were different levels of leadership development schools for both the enlisted and officers. And while I thought they did an extensive job up front, this still did not mean we did not have our share of ineffective supervisors, both enlisted and officers.

Once I joined the civilian sector, I found that in most cases (not all), the individual that is found to be the best individual contributor, worker in their department is usually tagged for management role, promotion, or is placed in the organization's succession plan. The key difference I noticed here was that those found to be a good individual contributor could be tagged for a leadership role without first attending some form of leadership development workshop so that they could be better prepared mentally and with the proper skillset for their new role.

Reflections from the workplace…

"I worked for someone that did not trust the team and was constantly questioning actions which in turn led to everyone's demotivation and low team morale. He also micro-managed us."—Viena Perez

For those placed on the organization's succession plan, they are usually provided a variety of development opportunities including leadership development workshops, 360 instruments to better understand themselves with input from others, high visibility projects, and other options. This is not always the case for those not on the Succession Plan.

While traveling through this professional journey of not only being in a managerial role but providing extensive development to others throughout my career be it educationally, through consulting, and/or coaching has brought me to this point. To the point of writing about what I believe new and existing leaders should reflect on, consider, and gain insight into so that they may be better at their role, and in turn positively impact those working for them and with them.

I am confident that you as a reader have at one time or another in your career have worked with someone difficult to work with. This reminds me of a comment I came across a while back, "All of us light up a room. Some when we walk in, others when we walk out. Which are you?" If we're honest with ourselves, at one time or another it may have been us that lit up the room when we walked out. Because we are having a bad day, had other issues on our mind, did not get a good night's sleep, did not buy into what we were working on, had personal issues on our mind, did not really know how to resolve the issue, or did not really like who were working with or trust them, among others.

It has also been noted that power negatively impacts empathy. A key and growing global leadership competency for leaders of today and going forward. By this, what has been found that as individuals rise in level of responsibility within organizations, they tend to be less empathetic to their workforce's issues. This was highlighted in a study by Deloitte (Volini et al., 2021), where they asked executives and their workforce to rank in priority order 10 items, one being "Improving worker well-being." The executives ranked it eighth, while not surprisingly the workforce ranked it third. Like two ships in the night and a total disconnect as to what was important to the workforce. This all took place in 2021, in the middle of the pandemic, when you would think leaders would be more sensitive to what their workforce (along with them) were going through.

Because of this, I have always said that I will always have a job for life. I say this because I have been educating and consulting on the topics of leadership, motivation, communications, diversity, empowerment, engagement, workplace experience, change, team development and dynamics, sexual harassment, and others. And while the topics have evolved over time, they are still more similar than different in many ways to where I began almost forty years ago. One example of this is that communications was a topic in leadership development workshops when I began. Today, communications or lack thereof is still an issue.

Another example of this is the following. I conducted my dissertation almost twenty years on the topic of leader-member exchange (LMX) in a virtual and co-located work environment (you'll see a model of this later in the book). In other words, I studied the relationship between leaders and their staff while working in a co-located (in the same office) or virtual (remote or hybrid).

Interestingly, the Pandemic made this a reality for many organizations, and some acted as if it was something new. Now in addition to interpersonal skills for leaders, organizations are also trying to arm their leaders with remote leadership skills. All of this is occurring, while the evidence keeps pointing to the fact that taking care of the employees makes not only good moral sense, but good business sense (Pfeffer, 2015).

So welcome to this book and let's begin the journey of what those soon to be, recently in, or with extensive experience in a managerial capacity should consider going forward.

Reflections from the workplace…

"My previous boss always asked how she could help us to be more efficient. She made everyone feel wanted."—Karian Tahbaz

---

The Journey in This Book

I will begin with the trends impacting and forcing organizations to change. This chapter will highlight what trends are taking place and the implications for organizations, the workplace, and their leaders.

I will then transition into what today's workforce is expecting. The sort of psychological contract that has come front and center in organizations around the world in today's workplace. The book will address the gap that seems to exist more often than not in the workplace between the workers and those in the managerial roles.

The next chapter will include some other workforce considerations. In particular, how the workplace continues to shift and change, and the continual growth needed by leaders to address these changes.

I will continue by highlighting the growth and implications of AI on organizational dynamics and the importance of HI during these changes.

I will also include a section in the book on the topic of neuroscience and leadership that has been growing in press, research, and significance. With the growing emphasis on the psychology of the workforce this piece will be fundamental for leaders to consider.

I will include a section for considerations to go from just being a BoSS to a better leader. It will not only spell out leader, but what each one means for consideration for the reader. Addressing what the implications will be for 21st century organizations and its leaders and workforce.

I will provide you some closing thoughts, considerations, and recommendations. I will end by providing some resources for you to consider using, while thinking of your workforce, and organization.

Throughout the book I will be inserting questions for you to consider. I will in addition include a piece with questions at the end for you to consider and reflect on as you come to the end of the book.

Last you will find 3 questionnaires to consider using, from an individual and potentially 360 perspective when it comes to what does to take to create a Human Intelligent (HI) Workplace, the second addressing your leadership effectiveness through a Leadership Behavior Effectiveness (LBE) questionnaire.

These are intended to have you pause, reflect, and possibly gather external perspectives in addition to yourself, while looking to improve yourself, your organizational people dynamics, and overall organizational environment. While you can use them individually, you will get the most value when you have others take the questionnaire(s). They are intended to help you and your organization help itself as you focus on this very important topic. Welcome to the BoSS and your reflective journey on improving your behaviors in a managerial role.

CHAPTER 1

CURRENT STATE OF ORGANIZATIONS: TRENDS WITH IMPLICATIONS FOR ORGANIZATIONS

ABSTRACT

This chapter describes the numerous trends taking place. These trends are causing organizations to adapt and change. The changing demographics along with the various growing multigenerational and multicultural changing workforce will force organizations to adapt and change or lose their human capital competitive edge. Those that adapt and provide effective leadership will create organizational cultures that are agile and continuing to evolve as societal changes occur around them.

There is also an increasing skills shortage that has only been made worse with the pandemic. This skills shortage along with the aging workforce and growing multigenerational workforce behind it will create opportunities and challenges for organizations and its leaders.

These trends will continue to evolve and more will appear forcing organizations to revisit their present paradigms. Leaders will need to become increasingly aware or educated on their unconscious biases. With growing changes comes challenges and opportunities. The organizations and leaders that not only acknowledge these trends and changes but adapt to them, will be in a better position to face the uncertain future that all organizations will have to face. Welcome to the 21st century workplace.

The BOSS for 21st Century Organizations, pages 17–26
Copyright © 2026 by Emerald Publishing Limited
All rights of reproduction in any form reserved.
doi:10.1108/978-1-80592-158-520251002

Keywords: Leadership; human intelligent workplace; human centered workplace environment; worker psychology; human capital trends; organizational environment

Change Is Inevitable...

Today's organization is in many ways dramatically different than what our parents and grandparents grew up working in. There are many changes taking place while expectations of today's worker are shifting. To say we are living in a *volatile, uncertain, complex,* and *ambiguous* (VUCA) times is probably an understatement. This was a term created by the military. While this is occurring, people are looking for more than just a paycheck today but for meaning, purpose, and fulfillment at work (Mackey & Sisodia, 2013).

Today's organizations are faced with several trends that are and will force organizations to adapt and change at a faster rate and have dramatic implications for new and upcoming leaders. Which means another potential way to consider VUCA is to view it from the perspective of having a *vision* of where the organization wants to go, to *understand* the challenges and opportunities, ensuring there is *clarity* of the goals and path forward, and that the organization through its workforce is *agile* in facing the changes.

Some tend to see the acronym VUCA to be dated. And so recently there is another acronym that some feel is timelier and more relevant. BANI which stands for Brittle, Anxious, Nonlinear, and Incomprehensible is seen by more to be a relevant acronym for today's organization (Kraaijenbrink, 2022). Irrespective of your preference for an acronym, most will probably agree that they capture the essence of what organizations, they're leaders, and workforce are facing today.

Bottom line is that the organizational culture that leaders create and enable can be one of glass half empty or half full. Those of you referred to as the boss will need to be open to innovation, demonstrate humility and not arrogance, listen not to respond but to understand, be empathetic which means I understand, and last be compassionate which translates into how I can help or here is how I can help.

The trends consist of the acceleration of change imposed on organizations due to a variety of issues including globalization. Organizations are having to change faster and be nimbler due to the increase in technology, an aging workforce, four (soon to be five) generations in the workplace, and an increasing diverse workforce especially in the US (Mouriño, 2014). All of these changes cannot be executed effectively without an engaged workforce that is supported and enabled by an effective leadership team.

Change is inevitable especially if when we realize that only 70 of the Fortune 500 companies that existed in 1955 still exist. As of today, more than 2000 companies have come and gone, and that the life expectancy of organizations is declining (Frank & Roehrig, 2014). All of we have to consider are the organizations that have disappeared since 2000, organizations like Borders Books, Blockbuster, and Circuit City who at one time was listed in the book *Good to Great* as a great company. These and other companies have disappeared. Since 2000 other companies have been created such as Amazon, Bing, Facebook, Starbucks, Uber, Pandora, and Netflix to just name a few. Some of these organizations like Uber, Amazon, and Airbnb are completely new and different business models.

Technology, globalization, aging demographics, diversity, multiple generations in the workplace, and changing expectations from today's workers are causing and in many cases forcing organizations to adapt and change at a faster rate than before. These reasons and probably more to come in the future are why most executives say that their organizations will change more in the next five years. And while change is not new as organizations constantly adapt their strategies, utilize new technologies to run more efficiently and increase productivity, and use mergers as a growth strategy, even some of these don't work and management is usually the culprit.

These organizational changes emphasize two points. One, that the traditional organizational model and framework that existed in the past is not necessarily going to make your organization successful in the future. The second point is that technology has changed the paradigm of how we work, where we work, on what we work on, with whom we work, and in turn has implications for the supervisor and employee relationships of the future.

Regarding technology and to put things in perspective, just consider that it took the radio 38 years, the TV 13 years, and the internet 4 years to reach 50 million people. Today we have more mobile devices then we have people on the planet. Technology has enabled the boss to work in different places then their workforce. It has also allowed more to work from home, hotels, and around the world and for organizations and employee workplaces to be more creatively designed (Berman, 2016).

As if it has not been difficult for those in a management position to manage their teams face to face, the increase in technology has now added a new challenge and opportunity when managing virtual teams because you can become the boss of a team that is virtual or co-located around the country or the world. Technology is transforming the way managers will supervise in the 21st century (Michelman, 2016). The implications for you are that how well you manage a potential virtual team by ensuring you have a trusting relationship (more on this topic later) with your team (regardless of where they are) can lead to an engaged and effective performing team and department (Gilson et al., 2015). Technology will be further enhanced with the now growth of Artificial Intelligence (AI). This will be discussed further in a later chapter along with the implications for the workforce and leaders.

The global workforce as we know it is aging today and will dramatically do so by 2030 (Strack, 2014). It is estimated that only two countries will have enough of a workforce for the future, these are Mexico and India. This is due to the number 2.1 which is what it will take to replace the present workforce. This entails immigration, emigration, births, and deaths (Coughlin, 2017). How organizations adapt to this changing and aging demographic will enable them to reinvent themselves going forward or not. Sticking to 20th century beliefs, behaviors, and practices that enable ageism will not be helpful.

Population aging, fueled by declining birth rates and increases in life expectancy, is a megatrend that will continue in the US and many other countries for the next several decades (Wilner Golden, 2022). This aging segment of society has created challenges and opportunities for organizations. The challenges consists of ageism as AARP has noted has been on an increase.

Aging, which one would believe should be a key component of any organization's diversity, equity, and inclusion strategy. Yet for more organizations than should be possible, the aging segment of the workforce is either an afterthought, or not a thought at all. One would believe that more organizations would pay particular attention to this trend, since the segment over 60 alone presents a $22 trillion market (Wilner Golden, 2022).

Not only is this aging segment of society a growing consumer market share but can continue to be a key segment of the workplace. This is particularly important when some of the key skills needed for today and tomorrow's workplace are critical thinking, empathy, listening, problem-solving, and relationship management, all skills found missing in new graduates, found in older workers, and needed particularly by leaders.

A Conference Board study found that many boomers plan to work on average through the age of 70 and many polled they may never retire. This study found that Boomers are working for numerous reasons, but the primary one is for financial reasons (Lombardo & Meyerson, 2024). Another study found that the fastest growing segment in the workforce are those over the age of 75 (Lucas, 2023). Both of these studies highlight that while ageism is alive in well in today's society and workplace, it is not stopping older members of society from continuing to work.

Leaders and organizations have an opportunity to take advantage of this growing segment of society and their workforce, by ensuring ageism is not part of the organizational culture. Yet a 2019 study of 10,000 organizations found that two-thirds of them considered older workers a *competitive disadvantage* (Bersin & Chamorro-Premuzic, 2019). This is an interesting study, since the aging demographic is not only the general workforce, but also in the leadership ranks as the average age of CEOs is almost 58.

As if this is not enough there will also be a skills shortage particularly in the Science, Technology, Engineering, and Math fields (Gordon, 2013). Presently, there is a half-million shortage in IT and computer science jobs, about the same for high end manufacturing, nursing shortage, commercial pilots, and others. This will increase competition for the limited workforce around the globe. Organizations will need to revisit their human resource policies when it comes to an aging workforce going forward. Leaders will need to address their own biases when it comes to an aging workforce.

Organizations now have for the first time in the history of postindustrial era have five generations in the workplace. Baby Boomers and Millennials have been receiving a lot of attention. Baby Boomers are retiring at the rate of 2 every 30 seconds. Millennials are positioned now to take over the majority of the workforce and by some have already become the largest portion of the workforce (Good, 2016). This will present opportunities and challenges leaders as they try to manage and lead the diversity of an intergenerational workforce.

Millennials are looking for their supervisors to be more engaged especially since as they more so than previous generations in the workforce value development and educational opportunities (Wolper, 2016). Millennials are also looking to their immediate supervisors to coach and provide more hands-on support without micromanaging (Campbell, 2016). Increasingly those in a leadership role are having to manage a more diverse workforce in addition to the growing female and diverse workforce with the additional complexity that the different generations bring to the workplace.

When it comes to diversity an increasing change is the growing diverse workforce in particular the Hispanic/Latino workforce, now and into the future. There were 53 million Hispanic/Latinos in the US, when Dr. Rodriguez first wrote his book Latino Talent (Rodriguez, 2008), today they are at 63 million making US the number two country in the world with most Latinos and Spanish speaking people. The US has more Latinos than Canada has Canadians or Spain has Spaniards.

In 2017 Latinos became the largest entrants into the US workforce. Latinos are expected to make up 78% of the new entrants into the workforce in this decade. Due to its young age as a demographic, it also makes up the largest portion of the Millennials, 44% (Krogstad et al., 2016). Every 30 seconds two non-Hispanics are eligible to retire while one Hispanic turns 18. This is one of the reasons why some feel that organizations cannot survive in the future without this growing demographic (Llopis, 2015).

The average age of Latinos is 27 while for the Anglo demographic it is 40 (Rodriguez, 2008). This segment of the US represents a $3.4 trillion purchasing power, or if it were a country it would be fifth in the world from a GDP perspective. They make up 25% of the US workforce and Latino businesses are growing 10 times faster than non-Latino businesses. The Society for Hispanic Engineers found that Latinos is the third fastest growing economy in the world. Unfortunately, this growing segment of the workforce is feeling underrepresented and overlooked (Sahadi, 2024).

This demographic shift creates a great opportunity for leaders to capitalize on their diverse workforce while working through the challenges of managing a growing workforce demographic that may approach their work differently (Rodriguez, 2008). The diverse workforce creates opportunities because organizations and leaders can capitalize on this growing workforce that might approach work situations from a different and fresh perspective.

This demographic change can also create challenges, because while not monolithic, Latinos tend to culturally respect authority versus challenge, and this can and has been seen at times as not aggressive enough. Latinos tend to instead of tooting their own horn model modesty more often and this can be seen as career oriented enough (Rodriguez, 2008). In summary, these changes are creating opportunities for those in managerial capacity to manage and lead differently.

The aging workforce is being followed by not only a growing multicultural growing workforce and consumer, but also by a growing skills shortage. One example is that commercial airline pilots have to retire by the age of 65 with an estimated shortage of 30,000 pilots by 2032. There is a nursing crisis, something made worse with the pandemic. In the technology realm, there is an estimated 500,000 shortage, along with manufacturing, and construction among others.

This skills shortage will cause increasing competition for the decreasing skilled workforce. As Mr. Aguh (former Chief Innovation Officer—U.S. Dept. of Labor) and Mr. Etzwilier (CEO Siemens Foundation) highlighted in the panel at the Conference Board's People 2030: Our Talent, Our Future conference, there will be labor shortages for the next 10 years, if not an always tight labor market (Aguh & Etzwilier, 2023). The question for your organization and your leadership, how is it working to address this challenge and differentiate itself?

And Then Came the Pandemic

All of these trends were already taking place before the Pandemic. Now things have dramatically changed, and I don't believe will be returning to business as usual. Everything mentioned previously has over the last couple of years been put on steroids. Organizations had to change and change quickly due to their workforce not being able to work in their offices. So, for those that could, and many could, they ended up working from home. The virtual, hybrid, and remote workforce is here to stay.

There have been those that say working remotely has a negative effect on organizational culture. The counter to this has been, culture was never about a building. It created the Great Resignation, Reassessment, Realignment, and Quiet Quitting among other terms that continue to be created.

As I've mentioned to my students while providing class remotely, now you can work anywhere in the world and never leave where you presently reside.

In addition, the number of retirees has dramatically increased due to the Pandemic. More work and pressure have been put on those remaining behind, particularly in the medical institutions like hospitals and educational institutions. Teachers have felt the extra work and stress while trying to teach remotely. In turn you're seeing more teachers leave the profession. This makes it increasingly imperative for organizations to reinvent themselves and create a more balanced, healthy, and engaging workforce. Because unfortunately this along with other occurrences may be another reason for the creation of the phenomena known as "quiet quitting." Some have described it as just doing enough to get by.

I mentioned previously that the workforce is aging. Recently it has been cited that since 2020, there were more 60-year old's than 5 years old's and that by 2035 there will be more 60-year old's than 18-year old's and turn into a $22 trillion opportunity for organizations globally (Golden). How organizations adapt to these changes and revisit policies and practices moving forward will be critical to their success. Recently, the US has been struggling with what to do with the shortage of pilots as many will be forced to retire due to many turning 65. There is a silver lining here and that is that most over 50 plan to continue to work (Coughlin), if only organizations can mitigate discriminatory practices and change their recruiting teams and hiring managers of the myths that exist when it comes to the older workforce (Taylor & Lebo) and ageism such as being less productive, more expensive, or not wanting ongoing development.

These myths seem to be sticking in some cases, as mentioned previously with the study where over 10,000 organizations that found that two-thirds considered having an older workforce a disadvantage (Bersin & Chamorro-Premuzic, 2019). Think of this, a segment of the workforce is seen as a competitive disadvantage because of their age. This when most organizations are run by older white male CEOs averaging 57 years in age. The stereotypes and myths about the older workforce continue just like those in younger generations. Recently the Conference Board did a study titled "The Multigenerational Workforce," where they found that ageism is seen both by the older workforce, Baby Boomers and with the younger Generation Z (The Conference Board, 2022).

While this segment of society can be a value to organizations, organizations will also have to adapt their organizational culture and leadership practices to having a more diverse younger workforce with the increase in Latinos, African Americans, Asians, more women, and LGBTQ segments of their workforce.

Organizations in different industries are and will continue to face a worker shortage, something further ignited by the pandemic. There is already a shortage in nurses, construction, IT and computer skills, high-end manufacturing, and other areas. This is also leading to a major retooling within America's workforce with an expectation that as of 2021 over 50% of the workforce will need retooling (Falzon, 2021).

While the pandemic is something of the past, the genie is out of the bottle, and it will not be able to be put back in again. There is a paradigm shift that organizations and its leaders now have to work through. Those in the boss position now must retool themselves with having a team working remotely, creating effective leader employee relationships in a virtual work environment, and truly engaging their workforce moving forward. The challenge and sometimes outdated paradigms still exist.

In 2022, Apple was instructing its workforce to return to the office. An organization that is usually seen as progressive, expecting to have their employees back in the office. This when most of its workforce do not want this. To further support this, a recent study conducted in 2022 found that 1 in 6 felt connected at work with the least being those in the office, 42% of those working on site felt least connected compared to 22% of those fully remote (Accenture, 2022). In actuality, numerous organizations reported their workforce was more productive while working virtually (Johansen et al., 2023). Numerous studies have found that productivity is better with remote workers than those in the office (Followan, 2023).

Yet there seems to be a major disconnect with what the workforce want and what leadership is expecting. Especially, when the workforce was mostly productive during the pandemic. So while there are some that believe the workers need to come back into the office, there is research that does not support the need. Irrespective, more and more organizations will need to ensure they're leaders know how to lead a remote/hybrid workforce going forward.

There is an increasing disconnect between what has been sold, as Return-to-office (RTO) is needed and good for the organization, its culture, and the reality by the perception of the workforce. Another study found that RTO practices, does not impact positively the performance of an organization, that the leaders might not believe it to be value-add, and that it negatively impacts employee satisfaction (Ding & Ma, 2023). In essence, for those that have claimed that it RTO is important for organizational culture, are reminded by others that culture was never about a building.

Another area that seems to be catching momentum and working with some is the 4-day work week. Some companies and countries have tried it with positive results. It turns out that a third of American companies have tried it as a way to address the workforce stress and burnout (Egan, 2024). As more try it and more research continues to come out on its success, the bias that some leaders might have against it become more difficult to oppose, similar to the RTO efforts.

The boss, from first line supervisor through CEO will now have to ensure they are creating a great work experience in a virtual environment that is engaging their workforce, truly listening to their teams, creating an organizational culture of belonging, purpose, happiness, and meaning (Mosely & Irvine). They will have to do this while also taking care of themselves. A study found that 40% of executives found an increase in work-related stress (Pickup, 2022). In this same article, the author highlighted the Global Culture Report which found 43% of leaders believe work is impacting their happiness in their personal lives.

This is not only important for leaders but for their workforce where work-related stress is impacting lives. In the book, *Dying for a Paycheck*, the author highlights that work is the fifth cause of death, due to stress (Pfeffer, 2018). How leaders take care of themselves and in turn create a workplace environment that the workforce is taking care of themselves will be important going forward.

Reflections from the workplace…

"My previous boss treated everyone with respect and was fair. We always knew what was expected."— *Mariano Estrada*

Today most workers are looking for real meaning at work that is essential to happiness and life satisfaction and can elevate productivity in organizations (Merisotis, 2020). By creating a positive employee experience, something the workforce is increasingly expecting, particularly after the pandemic, can increase employee engagement (Whitter). This will be paramount, particularly with what the societal issues have had on the workforce like the pandemic, social unrest, the dramatic changes and increasing stress in the workplace which has put work due to stress as the fifth cost of death (Pfeffer, 2018) and the increasing cost to organizations of over $7 trillion in not having an engaged workforce (Friedman, 2005).

It does not help that there seems to continue to be a disconnect with management teams and their workforce. In their book, *The Mind of the Leader*, Hougaard and Carter point out that in a study of 52,000 managers, 86% of them considered themselves a good example and an inspiration while 82% of the workforce saw their leadership teams as discouraging. There seems to be room for improvement here. I'm confident as you read this you will agree.

I end this chapter where it began, there are variety of trends changing and taking place in today's workplace. Constant and faster paced change, along with a changing workforce, and worker expectations are causing organizational leaders to reassess how to reinvent themselves in order to be viable in the 21st century.

Today and tomorrow's organizations will be different, and worker's expectations are changing from wanting more out of work then just work, while some organizations are either not paying attention to these changes or don't consider them as important (Mackey & Sisodia, 2013). In your role as a leader, you will be instrumental and key in ensuring you create a servant leadership mentality in order to reframe previous expectations from the workforce of one of "how can I get the most out of my staff," to one of "what can I do to help my employees be more effective and engaged."

Reflections from the workplace…

"I worked for someone that did not engage nor inspire his team. He just gave orders with a deadline and expectation to have it done."—Andres Diaz

---

Summary

There are numerous trends taking place. These trends are causing organizations to adapt and change. The changing demographics along with the various age groups and changing multicultural workforce will force organizations to adapt and change or lose their human capital competitive edge. Those that adapt and provide effective leadership will create organizational cultures that are agile and continuing to evolve as societal changes occur around them. These trends will continue to evolve and more will appear forcing organizations to revisit their present paradigms. Those organizations and leaders that acknowledge these trends and changes will be in a better position to face the uncertain future that all organizations will have to face. Welcome to the 21st century workplace.

CHAPTER 2

CURRENT STATE OF THE WORKFORCE: THE CHANGING PSYCHOLOGY OF THE WORKFORCE

As a leader, you have the power and responsibility to help your team members discover purpose and significance in their work.

Westover (2025)

ABSTRACT

This chapter looks at today's workforce and the different expectations that they have from their organizations and leaders. They are looking for purpose (irrespective of age and length in the workplace), happiness, autonomy, psychological safety, respect, to be listened to. They are looking for empathy and leaders that appreciate what they do and healthy relationships with those they work with and their leaders. In summary, they are looking for leaders to care about them and unfortunately more of those in a management position do not know how. The organizations and leaders that provide these will have a competitive edge over others. The organizations that focus on the humanity in their workforce has and will see positive bottom line implications. For this to happen they will need human-centered organizational cultures that positively impacts their workforce. Last, this is not just me saying this. There is extensive research that has come out and continues to come out on this topic.

Keywords: Leadership; human intelligent workplace; human centered workplace environment; worker psychology; human capital trends; organizational environment

The BOSS for 21st Century Organizations, pages 27–33
Copyright © 2026 by Emerald Publishing Limited
doi:10.1108/978-1-80592-158-520251003

27

As if the previously changing trends impacting organizations were not enough changes taking place, there is also the psychology of the present-day worker. Today and tomorrow's worker is looking to feel engaged in their workplace and looking for more of a positive experience. They are looking for something different than the phrase used by some managers of "how can I get the most out of my employees."

It is estimated that over approximately 76% of employees are neither engaged nor disengaged. In a recent study global study of almost a quarter of a million surveyed, appreciation for a job well done and a good relationship with their supervisor was seen as the top needs for employees (Strack, 2014). Gallup found that having an engaged workforce led to increased productivity, lower turnover, and less absenteeism, with higher profits (Gallup Consulting, 2008).

I think you might agree, that if leaders are primarily responsible for bottom line deliverables, then they'd focus on creating a positive workplace experience through an engaged workforce and effective leadership behaviors because this has been found to lead increased engagement and productivity.

These changes are creating the need for ongoing leadership development efforts for organizations across the globe. This is supported by the estimated billions of dollars spent by companies on leadership development and the fact that the majority of senior executives believe that the ability to develop its leaders will provide it a competitive advantage. And this is further supported by studies that show that challenges for organizations across the globe have is developing managerial effectiveness as their number one imperative (Gentry et al., 2015).

Unfortunately, these efforts have not always paid off and this is one of the reasons why companies like Zappos and others have tried in the past to operate in a managerless environment. By the way, it did not work long term, so managers are needed, now we just need to ensure they continue to learn how to add a human centered approach to their workforce.

In addition to this, managers have a 70% of variance in employee engagement. This when 30% of US and 17% globally are estimated to be engaged—Gallup. Effective leaders can create a more engaged workforce, while ineffective ones can create an unhealthy workplace experience and in turn impact the health of their workforce.

There is presently a need and opportunity for leaders to create an organizational culture where their workers can be more engaged. Wharton psychologist Adam Grant highlighted that the three biggest challenges facing workers today are employee motivation, workplace well-being, and Artificial Intelligence (AI) (Yildirim, 2023). He goes on to point out that since most of us spent the majority of our waking day at work, there is an inherent responsibility to improve the workplace experience.

This is further supported by research by Gartner that found that employees who work for effective managers were 15× more likely to be high performers, 13× more engaged, 3× more likely to stay with their current employer, and 12× higher physical and mental well-being. This while 54% of those in a managerial role are suffering from stress-related work (Gartner, 2023).

Another study by Gallup found a strong connection between engagement and organizational outcomes. They found that in organizations where the workforce is more engaged, there is 23% higher profitability, 18% higher productivity in sales, 64% higher in workplace safety, 66% higher in well-being, 81% lower absenteeism, and anywhere from 18% to 43% lower turnover among others (Spisak, 2023).

Something else that has increasingly become important, and a workplace issue is psychological safety. Amy Edmundson who has researched and written about this concept extensively defines psychological safety as, "a belief that one will not be punished or humiliated for speaking up with ideas, questions, concerns, or mistakes" (Edmondson, 2018).

She highlights in her book several examples one dating back to one of the Shuttle disasters, where a newer engineer thought he saw something not right before takeoff. He had planned to bring it up in a meeting. But he noticed others being shut down trying to bring up issues, so he felt it was better not to say anything, because he would not be listened to. Unfortunately, we now know how that environment impacted the final result. This in an organization where safety was one of its organizational values. This example support what has been found, that when psychological safety is low not only will it impact team performance but also organizational performance (Lynn & Sarro, 2022).

When leaders don't focus on their workforce, it can lead to unfavorable results. For example, a Gallup study found that only 23% of employees trust their leaders, while 23% of employees felt they get the right amount of recognition. This when as mentioned earlier from a Boston Consulting Group study in their Ted Talk 2030 Workforce Crisis, in a global study of 200,000 participants found that the number one thing employees were looking for in their next potential employer was appreciation.

This unfortunately leads to the following, that 51% of employees are actively searching for a new job. And last, that only 2 out 10 employees feel connected to their organization (Yi, 2023). Bottom line, leaders that focus on creating an organizational environment where the workforce is engaged pays dividends, creates a great work experience, and in turn improves the bottom line, which is the focus of those in a managerial role.

Reflections from the workplace...

"I once worked for someone who after I had established (not meaning to) a reputation of being a difficult employee, he gave me a second chance. He basically said, we start here on a new page and what you've done in the past, is in the past. I went out of my way to do well, and it ended up being a very positive experience and opportunity to turn myself around."

The Conference Board in one of its Insights Brief, presented a paper titled: *Creating a More "Human-Centered" Workplace to Address Service and Manufacturing Labor Shortages* (Erickson et al., 2023), where they highlight an organization like Kohler looking to address some of these challenges and opportunities. Kohler has been investing in the employee experience by requesting feedback and responding to it (what a novel idea). They have focused on creating a stronger sense of belonging for their workforce in order to reduce turnover, which can costs from 150% of a person's salary and up.

This is of particular importance because we've learned that when a leader excludes anyone from participating in any sort of work activity, or contributing at work, it can make them feel uncomfortable at a minimum. As a leader you are responsible for achieving results through others and positively impacting the bottom line, then why not create an environment that can positively impact the workplace through your workforce, and in turn organizational success. Research continues to show us that when employees feel engaged and supported in their work they are more productive, innovative, and committed to the organization (Westover, 2025).

As you assess the human capital trends taking place and the changing psychology of the workforce, a consideration to be made is how well prepared is my workplace? How effective am I as a leader and our leadership team modeling the behaviors needed for these changing times? Is our organization practicing human intelligence through dignity, respect, and engaging our workforce in an effective manner in order to position our organization for success?

So much has been said and written about the impact and role that technology and in particular AI will play in the workplace (more of this later). But it is my position, that irrespective of the growth and impact of AI, it will be Human Intelligence (HI) that will still play a major role in the organization through leadership practices which in turn will impact the organizational culture and create either a great worker experience or not.

The following studies highlight the importance of leadership effectiveness. A study in 2021 by Deloitte in their Global Human Capital Trends survey, asked both executives and their workforce to rank order from importance to least important 10 items. With 1 being the most important and 10 being the least. One of the items was "improving employee well-being." The executives ranked this item eighth, while the workforce ranked it third. Like two ships in the night, completely different perspectives on the importance of issues in the workplace for the workforce. Is this because these two groups are not speaking and engaging in a heartfelt dialog about what is important for today's workforce? Or is it as some have pointed out that leaders tend to lose their empathy as they grow in a leadership capacity?

Part of this might be what has been highlighted as a three-part problem that organizations have with leadership. One is the inability to distinguish between confidence and competence, the second is our love for charismatic individuals, and the last is the allure of narcissistic individuals (Chamorro-Premuzic, 2020). The author highlights that what organizations should be doing is promoting individuals who demonstrate competence, humility, and integrity. He believes this might help in our journey to have better equipped individuals in a leadership role. I believe this can also lead to more humanistic and engaging workplaces.

These previous examples highlight the sometimes different perceptions from leaders and their workforce. This seems to support what has been highlighted in the past, that as an individual grows in rank in their organization, they tend to lose their empathetic qualities, something increasingly needed in today's growing human-centered workplace.

Reflections from the workplace…

"I worked for someone that had little interest in me as an employee or personally. He would email me at 3 a.m. and did not give full autonomy."

Workers today are expecting more from their workplace and leaders. Unfortunately, a majority seem to have an unhealthy relationship with their workplace (HP Research, 2023). In this study, of over 15,000 across 12 countries, HP found that only 27% of the workforce say they have a healthy relationship with their workplace. Over 80% are willing to earn less to be happier. Over 10% would take a pay cut to work for a leader who is empathetic and creates an engaging workplace experience.

The work environment has been noted as one that can have an impact on the worker's health. It has been estimated that health-care expenditures are in excess of $180 billion (Pfeffer, 2018), with those in management having a bigger impact on their workforce than their doctors. Bottom line today's workforce is expecting more from their organizations and leaders. This is something that AI will not be able to address, but effective leaders can by creating a human intelligent (HI) workplace in order to have a competitive human edge. In the last section of this book, you will find the HI questionnaire to use individually, with your team, or as an organization.

As highlighted in a Deloitte study, in order for an organization to make a shift from "survive to thrive, depends on an organization becoming distinctly human at its core – a different way of being that approaches every question, every issue, and every decision from a human angle first." (Volini et al., 2021). As organizations continue to evolve and with it an increase in technology, we need to remember that effective leadership behaviors and creating more human focused organizations will better position our organizations, workforce, and you the leader for success.

The research is clear. Taking care of your workforce is not a touchy-feely issue. It is a business imperative. Figure 2.1 highlights a sampling of the many books and the organizations such as Conference Board (of which I am a Senior Fellow on), Pew, Gallup, and others that continue to highlight the continual shift in the changing expectations from today and tomorrow's workforce. I have read all of these books and found the theme to be throughout that human-focused organizations will be increasingly important and viable for the workforce.

Summary

This chapter looked at today's workforce and the different expectations that they from their organizations and leaders. They are looking for purpose (irrespective of age and length in the workplace), happiness, autonomy, psychological safety, respect, to be listened to. They are looking for empathy and leaders that appreciate what they do and healthy relationships with those they work with and their leaders. In summary, they are looking for leaders to care about them and unfortunately more of those in a management position do not know how.

The organizations and leaders that provide these will have a competitive edge over others. The organizations that focus on the humanity in their workforce has and will see positive bottom line implications. For this to happen they will need human-centered organizational cultures that positively impacts their workforce. Last, this is not just me saying this. There is extensive research that has come out and continues to come out on this topic.

Figure 2.1

Research Makes the Case.

Source: Author's own.

CHAPTER 3

SOME OTHER WORKFORCE CONSIDERATIONS: THE EVER-CHANGING WORKPLACE

ABSTRACT

The following chapter covers those in a managerial role, from front line supervisor through senior executive need to reflect on their effectiveness and what today's workforce is expecting. If they believe they are effective, does this align with how their teams perceive them. If they are truly being effective, how do they know? And if they don't know, why not? While an individual in a managerial capacity needs to both manage and lead, I have found many more managing and few leading. As you read this chapter truly reflect and consider ways to confirm your perception on your effectiveness as not just a manager, but a leader. Today and tomorrow's workforce is expecting a leader who demonstrates effective leadership by listening, empathizing, ensuring her/his team is engaged, and that the organizational culture is one that is seen by others as healthy. Is your organization ready, are you?

Keywords: Leadership; human intelligent workplace; human centered workplace environment; worker psychology; human capital trends; organizational environment

Having worked for and with numerous supervisors, managers, directors, and executives over the years I wonder if they have ever thought how they will be remembered? You as the boss, will be one of many that people will work with over their work life span. What you might consider asking yourself is how will you be remembered by your staff? Will they remember you as

The BOSS for 21st Century Organizations, pages 35–43
Copyright © 2026 by Emerald Publishing Limited
doi:10.1108/978-1-80592-158-520251005

having treated them indifferently or as one who made them feel important, treated them with dignity and respect, and even when they make mistakes (which they will, just like you), did you help them course correct without treating them in a demeaning manner. Will you care how they feel about you? I ask this question not to be disrespectful, because there is too much research highlighting that many in the workplace believe their manager does not care. How you treat them will set the stage and context in the leader-employee working relationship and in turn can make a difference.

This is particularly important when there more times than needed a disconnect between what leaders believe and what the workforce experience as noted by the second piece in the entry to this chapter as you can see in the cited data above. Along with this there was a recent study found that only 25% of those surveyed considered their leaders to be engaging, passionate, and inspire the best from their workforce (Green, 2024). How can this continue in this day and age, when workers have different expectations from their leaders? Some of this may be due to what has been found as the decreasing lack of empathy as individuals go up the management chain.

There may be other issues at play as the following research highlights. Josh Bersin pointed out that 87% of employees feel highly productive while only 12% of leaders have confidence their team is productive. This while 65% of employees say they have taken on additional responsibilities (Bersin, 2023). In another study, Gallup found that only half of US workers knew what was expected of them (Gallup, 2024). Another in a series of examples of a leadership-workforce disconnect. This same study found that when managers are engaged, their employees also tend to be engaged.

To make the point above even more relevant, I was once making a presentation to a group of executives and asked them to rank how well they believe they individually were at communicating and listening and having quality conversations, to rate how they felt their overall management team was, and to rate how they felt their workforce would rate management in this area. I asked them to use 1–5 scale, with 1 being ineffective, 3 being average, and 5 being effective. Not surprisingly, they ranked themselves individually better or 4.3 on a 1–5 scale, while they rated their management at 3.8 and last, they thought the workforce would rate management at 3.5. In other words, as an executive group, I'm good, our management needs some work, and our workforce really believes they need work.

Bottom line, the results highlighted here that they believe they as executives are individually doing better than the rest of the management team and the workforce ranks management even lower. How can there be such a disconnect? Have they even thought of checking this information out? These executives seemed to forget they play an important role as a model for their managers and organization. As you read this a more important question to ask yourself, how would you rate yourself, your management team, how would your workforce rate your management team, how would they rate you?

Organizations and their Human Resources departments should not only continue to ensure they are positioning their executives for success but all of their managers. One way to address this is to ensure they are developing those that step into a management role for the first time. In the book, "The first 90 days" the author points out that in order to position yourself for success as a new boss you should "hit the ground running" and that your transition toward success begins as soon as you're aware of your new role and runs through your 90th day in your new role (Watkins, 2003). As the old saying goes, you only have one chance for a first impression.

So, while individuals in your organization may have an impression about you from your previous role and what you did, your new role as a supervisor now makes you responsible for achieving results not through your efforts but now by the efforts of others. You will need to change your approach and behaviors in your leadership role. And for those that have been in a leadership role, as you transition to your new position, you bring with you previous reputation in your earlier leadership role.

More organizations are being presented with the possibility of creating a workplace that becomes a human-centered organization, especially as the workforce is expecting this type of environment. A human-centered organization has been described as one that focuses on improved human experiences, is focused and cares about the experience of its diverse workforce and customers and builds innovation and continuous learning.

Something that more organizations than needed, are still coming up short to achieve (IBM study), especially with the changing psychology and expectations of today's workforce. In spite of some coming up short or due to this human-centered focus some have even suggested what organizations need to improve in this space, such as encouraging communications, developing empathy, building relationships, and leading by example among others (Knotts, 2023). Because when this is not done, it can lead to low engagement which has been found to be a $8.9 trillion lost in global GDP (Gallup, 2024). This should be important since being in a leadership role you're in front of ensuring there is a positive impact to the organization's bottom line.

Another point to remember is that in order to enable the above you need to not only focus on your behavior and your team, but your managerial colleagues. Because what does not help an organization and its workforce if only some leaders are effective. One way to do this, is by minimizing the silos in organizations and remember that as someone in a management role you gain more authority when you focus on the interdependencies with other managers and departments. This will better position you to earn respect, trust, and influence with others in your role as a leader (Hill, 2007).

As someone in a leadership role you will be involved in a multi-role capacity. You will have interpersonal roles that include serving as a figure-head, leader, and liaison; informational roles that consist of serving in a monitor, disseminator, and spokesperson; and decisional roles that include serving as an entrepreneur, disturbance handler, resource allocator, and negotiator (Mintzberg, 1975). A lot of things to keep in mind as a leader. And accepting this you might want to ask, what will you need to do to position yourself, your team, and your organization for success?

I have asked college students in my classes, how many want to be in a leadership role, and almost always, several raise their hands. My advice to them is, be careful what you wish for. Because when I've asked those in managerial roles, how it is to be in a leadership role, most if not all, allude to how difficult the role can be. That sometimes leading department staff members and workers can be difficult is an understatement. Which is probably 35% would forgo a pay raise to see their boss fired (Hougaard et al., 2018).

How you as a leader address conflict when it arises along with any other issues that may arise can increase everyone's stress. You in a leadership role are responsible for addressing these in a positive way. Remember you are always under the spotlight and how you manage your emotions can be contagious. This is probably why when faced with the stress that comes with a management role, there has been an increase in some considering returning to an individual contributor role if they could (Pickup, 2022).

Something as a leader you should consider is to do more listening and less talking. This has been seen as a need by the authors of "The Mind of a Leader," where they highlighted a study that found that only 8% of leaders were seen as effective listeners and communicators (Hougaard et al., 2018). This means leaders need to ensure they are listening to understand versus to respond. To make matters more difficult Gallup found that out of those managers that had conversations with their workers, only 16% of the workers found the conversation meaningful (Gallup, 2024). Would you consider yourself part of this 16%? I have found that most leaders do, which cannot be possible statistically.

Trying to be more effective at listening allows you as a leader to take time to learn more about each of your team members from an individual perspective. To have one-on-one conversations with each of your team members and learn what they have seen go well and not so well. To learn about your team member's aspirations and individual hopes. In essence to learn more about your team at a personal level. In summary, to listen to understand versus to respond.

In addition, you should gain insights from your own boss, especially since this is individual that selected you to be the new department boss. Assuming he or she is a good role model. Because sometimes those above you as I have alluded to earlier are not exactly the best of bosses. If you are taking over a department, function or organization, you might consider, if possible, to meet with the previous leader of the department. This individual will have a unique perspective on the opportunities and challenges of the department, team, and clients.

You should also meet with clients of the department or organization since this is a key constituent that have needs to be met. After all, serving these clients is why the department that you inherited exists. As the leader you should also meet colleagues and teams that have interdependencies with your department, function, or organization. You should have all of these meetings and discussions with the goal of gaining insights into the perception by others. This along with information of what has worked well before and might need improvements going forward will be invaluable for you as you step into your new area of responsibility.

As the boss you need to keep in mind that the role you have stepped into is both complex from an operations and human dynamics perspective. The department, function, or organization has been running in a certain way, with a culture enabled in part by the previous leader. Culture has been described as "the accumulated shared learning of a given group" (Schein, 1992). Culture includes the non-visible aspect of a department and organization. Culture encompasses the behavioral, emotional, and psychological aspects of a group usually influenced by its leader. No where do you find that organizational culture consists of a building, which is the argument made against those that say that they have to bring back their workforce into the office, since it might impact their organizational culture. This is especially relevant with the point made earlier that only one in six is committed with the least being those working onsite.

Now as a department supervisor or manager, function, or organizational executive in your role of you as a leader to take the entity to next level regarding operations and assessing the team you have inherited to see if you have the right team with the right skills in order to move forward. In essence placing your fingerprints on the department's culture and environment and creating one through your leadership philosophy and behaviors.

Reflections from the workplace…

"An effective behavior that I have seen from my boss was by providing training and coaching to new employees. He stressed how important it was for our group of waiters/employees to rely on effective teamwork and collaboration to carry out productive dinner services. He gave us constructive feedback on our performance and consistently complemented our individual contributions to each service."

What this leads to is departmental change which is a key role for you as the new leader. With change comes uncertainty, insecurity, and resistance by some. Some reasons given for individuals resisting change has been because they don't understand it, don't like it, or don't like the individual driving the change (Maurer, 2010), which in this case is the boss.

Much has been written about organizational change and why organizations need to adapt and evolve in a constantly changing global environment. In this day and age, organizations are striving to adapt and survive in what has become an uncertain and constantly changing work environment. This amount of change raises the dramatic need for constant communications and listening. Communications, something that has constantly been demonstrated as being underutilized when an organization or department is going through change (Kotter, 2007).

As a leader you need to be aware that there are certain key points you should keep in mind when it comes to enabling change. In doing so it might help you and team and minimize frustration and inefficiencies. In order to improve your chances of success as a leader when implementing some form of change you ought to consider in addition to providing leadership support that you are addressing the following key components (Donnelly, 2023).

You should:

1. articulate the vision of the future, if not team members will be confused as to what the end goal is supposed to look like.
2. ensure your team members have the right skills, because if not you could have a group of anxious team members since they are not sure how to accomplish the new tasks and with whom.
3. ensure you have created an incentive for the change, because if not this could lead to gradual change.
4. ensure your team members have the right resources in order to minimize frustration.
5. make sure there is an action plan in order to minimize false starts.

All of these can be best addressed by communicating, listening, and engaging your team. Because at the end of the day, in your leadership role your goal is to get work done through others and not on your own. And for the reader that thinks, I sort of know this and this is too fundamental. I would ask you then how effective may others be perceiving you as demonstrating these behaviors? Do you know this for sure? How have you confirmed this? I would not be highlighting all of the research that keeps finding a disengaged, stressed workforce that might be looking for a better opportunity if part of the problem is how effective are those in a leadership role. As you reflect and assess yourself, try to be honest with yourself and look to gain other's insights and perceptions. Not to create an imposter syndrome in you, but to help you help yourself through reflection, observation, dialog, engagement with your team, and in turn behavior change if needed. Remember leadership is about continual learning, it is a journey, not a destination.

As you either begin or continue in your role as the boss, (irrespective of first line supervisor, mid-level manager, or executive), through your behaviors, actions, and demeanor you begin to establish your brand and people begin to create a perception of you as an individual, leader, and overall boss. Fundamental to all of this is establishing trust and credibility with all of the stakeholders mentioned before, especially your staff and team.

Over the years, in conducting many leadership development workshops, I've always asked the participants to provide me a list of effective characteristics of someone they have worked for that they would work for again. The following is just a sample, but the first one is the one that has come up in all of the sessions that I have conducted. Trust is also "one of the most studied variables in the virtual team literature" (Gilson et al., 2015).

Trustworthy	Listener	Knew their job
Collaborator	Communicator	Inspirational
Ethical	Compassionate	Personable
Approachable	Humility	Motivator
Team Oriented	Empathetic	Visionary

Most leaders and even an experienced ones, will not have all of these characteristics. But this does not mean they should not reflect on the above to ensure they are demonstrating some of these and work on the ones that they know they need to improve. Empathy and compassion have become even more prominent today, which means as a leader I understand, and I want to help or how can I help.

Fundamental to all of this is good listening, something most consider ourselves pretty good at. But if we're honest with ourselves, due to all of multiple priorities that we're faced with, more times than not there are those that tend to listen to respond than to understand. Partly, because we have a brain that tries to be efficient and our attempt at supposedly multitasking, which research tells us impacts our effectiveness, memory, our health and even IQ.

Those in a leadership role should be aware that they will need both good management skills and demonstrate good leadership behaviors. The ones highlighted above are usually associated with the leadership side (or soft skill) of being a boss and both will be instrumental to success. If those that truly want to be an effective leader, they should consider working to make their department one where the staff are happy to work in and happy to work for their leader. Because not only has extensive research backed this up, but if all of us reflect on a time when we were happy at work, the boss plays a fundamental role.

This can be done if you as a manager really get to know your people, enable your employees to know each other, help them to reward each other, provide positive feedback, and ensure everyone understands the organization (Burg, 2016). The last thing a manager wants to do is not motivate their workforce by behaving in ways that minimize an engaging environment, such as micromanaging as I have seen more than my share, and in most cases, they do not believe they are micromanaging.

As a leader your role will be to engage your staff particularly during these changing times. The future of work is one where people will change jobs often, there will be an increase in a contingent workforce, technology will continue to change the way we do work, and organizational structures will need to be flatter and agile (Bersin, 2016). Your opportunity and challenge will be to make your department and/or organization a great place to work.

So, Do I Manage, or Do I Lead?

> You manage things and lead people…

Peter Drucker, considered by some as one of the founding fathers of modern management has been credited with the following line "Management is doing things right; leadership is doing the right things." Another way to consider this and what it means for you as a leader is that you consider that management looks to address the more tactical and task related issues such as delegation, organizing, and providing direction while leadership should provide more of the people aspect of a manager such as influencing, collaborating, motivating, inspiring your team to achieve their results. Managers are about the business of the operations and results or "the what," while leadership addresses the diversity, ingenuity, and people aspect "or how" of the job (Perrin, 2010). Or as has been highlighted before, you lead people and manage things.

You need to be good or work to be effective from both perspectives. As a leader you need to be able to ensure you're engaged (as needed without micromanaging) and managing to the deliverables of the team and at the same time inspiring or leading your team to bigger and greater engagement and in turn the department results.

Summary

Those in a managerial role, from front line supervisor through senior executive need to reflect on their effectiveness and what today's workforce is expecting. If they believe they are effective, does this align with how their teams perceive them. Executives interestingly have a more positive view of their effectiveness. They are in a position to create a healthy organizational climate in partnership with their managerial teams. Today's workforce expectations has different expectations from their leaders. They want an engaging workplace experience. Engagement costs and those in a leadership role can impact positively or negatively. So while you need to manage and lead, I have found many more managing and few leading. What about you? Today and tomorrow's workforce will require effective leadership. Is your organization ready, are you?

CHAPTER 4

ARTIFICIAL INTELLIGENCE (AI) + HUMAN INTELLIGENCE (HI) = EFFECTIVE WORKPLACE

ABSTRACT

This chapter looks to address the constant change of technology and its impact on the workplace. Artificial Intelligence (AI) is and will be having an impact on their workforce. In spite of the growth of AI, research continues to demonstrate that going forward organizations will need to focus on their human intelligence from their leaders as expected from their workforce. AI will not totally eliminate the need for the human touch. Leaders will need to focus on their interpersonal skills going forward. Listening, empathy, collaboration, creativity, innovation, and the psychology of today's workforce will require these. The organizations and their leaders that focus on the human aspect of work will create a competitive edge.

Keywords: Leadership; human intelligent workplace; human centered workplace environment; worker psychology; human capital trends; organizational environment

There are some who believe that Artificial Intelligence (AI) will lead to things as seen in the movie Terminator and create apprehensions. Only the future will tell. What we know is that AI has been around for some time. However, recently with the exposure of ChatGPT among others, AI has taken a more prominent role.

There are numerous concerns among different segments of society on the implications of the over dependence on AI. From college professors

The BOSS for 21st Century Organizations, pages 45–49
Copyright © 2026 by Emerald Publishing Limited
All rights of reproduction in any form reserved.
doi:10.1108/978-1-80592-158-520251006

concerned about students using ChatGPT to write papers for them, to fake bots, marketing, political ads, and other inappropriate uses of the technology. Some organizations are even using emotion-tracking AI to detect employees' feelings (Andalibi, 2024).

One of the bigger concerns is the elimination of jobs and in turn implications for today's workforce. In addition to this question, is the one of will AI fix work? How will AI impact leadership and its collaboration with its workforce? All interesting questions that eventually we'll have answers in a not-so-distant future. AI has really taken off and due to this, some 11% and expected to grow to 21% of mid-size and large companies have or will hire a Chief Artificial Intelligence Officer (Kulp, 2024).

However, if history is any indicator, that concern might be a misplaced. In the Industry 4.0 report it showed that with the creation and explosion of the PC between 1980 and 2015, it displaced 3.5 million jobs, but it created 19.5 million new jobs. The World Economic Forum reports indicated that the growth of AI will create a job growth of 69 million jobs and a decline of 83 million jobs (2023 Future Jobs Report). Others believe AI will cause the elimination or change of different jobs; some believe up to 40% of jobs (Reed, 2024).

Still others estimate that by 2030 30% of hours worked across the US economy could be automated and this will lead to an expansion of workforce development and hiring (Ellingrud et al., 2023). However, the one area I don't believe it will eliminate is leadership, even though it will impact it just as it will impact other areas of work and organizations overall. As is highlighted in the article about leaders and AI, the authors make the case that they don't believe the best leaders will be replaced by AI as long as they focus on honing their capabilities in awareness, compassion, and wisdom (Hougaard et al., 2024).

While this may seem alarming to some or serve as an awakening, we need to remember some of the jobs are related to repetitive types of lower skilled work and it also means there will be a growing need for reskilling. We won't really know, until organizations start implementing their AI technical strategic initiatives. However, as of May 2023, almost 4,000 jobs were displaced by AI.

All of this reskilling is further accentuated with the fact that as of today the average half-life of skills is now less than five years which is why it is enabling organizations to use reskilling as a strategic imperative (Tamayo et al., 2023). Add to this that during the pandemic human attributes such as friendship, empathy, and curiosity were front and center, all attributes that up to now AI does not possess (Kissinger et al., 2021). And empathy has become a fundamental competency for leaders.

Irrespective of how the change occurs, it will impact the way work in the future. Presently, 64% of employees are struggling finding time and energy to get their work done. There are 70% who believe with the help of AI they will delegate as much work as possible. And twice the number of leaders have indicated that AI will provide value in productivity versus cutting head-count. Some have even proposed that AI can do a better job of management and leadership than humans (Van Quaquebeke & Gerpott, 2023).

While some might scoff at this notion, let us not forget that the concepts of communications, listening, empathy, respect, and just plain treating our workforce with respect which is human, is not a new concept and has been researched and written about since last century. But here we are, still writing and research coming out about the need for leaders to create quality human focused organizations and yet we still have a large segment of the workforce disengaged due to those in management not being as effective as needed.

In addition to this, there is the workforce reskilling perspective. It is expected that AI will enable, maybe even force a change in the way 65% jobs are done by 2030 (Learning – LinkedIn, 2024). This is particularly important when it has been noted in this study that it is 2.5× more expen-sive to hire a new employee than it is to reskill your present workforce, this when it has been estimated that 82% employees will need new skills in the era of AI.

As mentioned previously in this book, the interpersonal skills will be fun-damental for tomorrow's workforce. Something that the aging workforce mentioned earlier in this book tends to have honed over their career. The World Economic Forum indicates that almost half of the employees will need reskilling in this decade and some highlighted are empathy, listening, self-awareness, life-long learning, and leadership among others (Winkle-Giulioni, 2024). This will not only be important for your workforce but especially for you as a leader.

Some have written that there might be a mistake and fallacy in comparing AI to human intelligence (Wayas, 2023). In this article, the author highlights that while AI may not be able to as creative or empathetic like humans, it can still do these tasks, just differently. The article closes with the point that AI will not only effect blue collar workers but also white collar and in turn organizations should consider upskilling their workforce.

Yet here are, with millions of dollars being spent and invested into leader-ship development and still we have discrimination, intimidation, or other bad behaviors being demonstrated by those in management. This is not to say that AI will totally eliminate this. After all AI is a creation made by imperfect human beings with their biases and flaws. But now AI is in the con-versation for its role in management. There are some that have connected AI to leadership (Smith & Green, 2018). The authors make the point that potentially sometime in the future, those in a leadership role will have a new follower and that follower will be the AI machine. This shift will potentially lead to a paradigm shift in the future workplace.

AI will have an impact and we will learn more as time and AI progresses. But in the meantime, reskilling will need to be a strategic imperative for organizations and their workforce. This initially seems like a positive implication, since in The Puzzle of Motivation Ted Talk, it was highlighted that one key motivational factor for the workforce is Personal Mastery, or the ongoing need for continual development. We will learn more as time progresses and as AI matures and organizations look to integrate the technological changes into their organizations similar to what occurred as the PC became more integrated into the fabric of how organizations worked.

With all these changes that organizations are facing, you are embarking on a journey of enabling your staff, team, department, function, or organization to one that is great to work for. You as the leader will have plenty of influence here. You are like a pebble in a lake, you either create ripples or worse. What sort of impact do you want to have as the boss, whether you are a front-line supervisor, middle manager, or executive? It all depends on how you behave, what you demonstrate, and what you are willing to continue to learn, as leadership is all about lifelong learning.

The future is unknown and while we can speculate, those in a leadership role have to model a belief that the future will be better. That at a minimum our organizations will evolve with the growth of technology in particular AI as organizations have in the past with the changes that have come before and that you as a leader will help the workforce adapt and grow with these changes.

Thomas Malone has been credited with saying:

> We have spent way too much time thinking about people *versus* computers, and not nearly enough time thinking about people and computers. Way too much time thinking about what jobs computers are going to take away from people, and not nearly enough time thinking about what people and computers can do together that could never be done before.

This is further supported by research that finds certain leadership behaviors in the interpersonal space are going to be an imperative for the workforce in the era of AI (Smith & Green, 2018). In the era of AI, human intelligence (HI) will be part of the fabric of organizations for the success of all.

Again, if history is an indicator, as mentioned earlier, previous technological advancements have created change. But instead of new versus old ways of doing business and work, it can be more of what we have seen which is how do we complement each other and make a difference going forward. Leaders will be key in these changes not only by modeling what they expect but also providing a sense of psychological safety for the workforce to accept the changes that AI will bring.

We have to ensure that the workforce understands the "why" for the change or technological evolution. Our brain is wired to be on the lookout for threats and sometimes new things such as technology or any sort of change creates a threat. Leaders need to model and enable a partnership with the workforce integrating into the fabric of the organization this new technology and chapter in the life of organizations.

Summary

AI is and will be having an impact on their workforce. In spite of the growth of AI, research continues to demonstrate that going forward organizations will need to focus on their human intelligence from their leaders as expected from their workforce. AI will not totally eliminate the need for the human touch. Leaders will need to focus on their interpersonal skills going forward. Listening, empathy, collaboration, creativity, innovation, and the psychology of today's workforce will require these. The organizations and their leaders that focus on the human aspect of work will create a competitive edge.

CHAPTER 5

NEUROSCIENCE AND NEUROLEADERSHIP = SMART BOSS

Our brain needs a leader to create environments that feel safe and certain. Needs leaders who communicate well, make understanding them easy, create fair and transparent processes, so our brains do not waste precious effort in second guessing or trying to understand what to do next. (Swart et al., 2015)

ABSTRACT

Neuroscience and Neuroleadership continue to gain research and insights as further research, and books keep getting written about it. While fairly new to the concept of leadership, more research is highlighting its importance. Just like Emotional Intelligence gained prominence in the 20th century, these concepts are highlighting for leaders and their workplace the importance of what is going on inside our brains when dealing with each other, at work, and the implications of leadership. The growing importance of these concepts in the workplace, where humans work and will spend most of their adult waking hours (estimated to be 90,000), and cultures are created will continue to play a role with particular focus on leaders.

Keywords: Leadership; human intelligent workplace; human centered workplace environment; worker psychology; human capital trends; organizational environment

The BOSS for 21st Century Organizations, pages 51–59
Copyright © 2026 by Emerald Publishing Limited
All rights of reproduction in any form reserved.
doi:10.1108/978-1-80592-158-520251007

The above comment highlights why there is a growing emphasis on neuroscience and neuroleadership work. The one about people wanting to be valued has been highlighted in a study by Boston Consulting Group in the Ted Talk 2030 Workplace Crisis and how to begin solving it. In it they found that the number one thing people wanted in their future employer was to be appreciated. This too has neurological underpinnings.

From a neuroscience perspective what we need to keep in mind (no pun intended) is that depending on how a leader makes an employee feel will impact their emotions and in turn their actions. If an employee feels a bond with their leader then it generates serotonin in the brain and in turn helps the employee feel trustful of them and helps in their relationship. When a leader shows support and trust in their workers, dopamine is generated and the worker feels confident, and enthusiasm needed for problem solving. And when a task is finally accomplished with support from their leader, this generates Oxytocin which helps create feelings of relief and accomplishment (Swavely, 2020).

The above and other research makes me wonder why some in leadership have tried to minimize the use of feelings in the workplace, in some cases considering it a disadvantage, particularly when making decisions. Especially when neuroscientists have found that feelings inform and influence our thoughts and decisions, not the other way around (Watz & Mason, 2019). And with as many decisions that are made by humans on a daily basis, this takes an increased importance. As a leader reflect on your daily decisions and how they may be affected when you or your team are under stress or conflict?

There is also an increase in research when it comes to neuroscience and trust. It has been found that creating an employee-centric culture is good for business with trust being fundamental (Zak, 2019). It has also been found that in high trust organizations workers tend to be more productive, collaborative, and overall happier with their lives. The research makes an impressive case for employee-centric and high trust organizations. In these companies 74% report less stress, 106% more energy, 50% more productive, 13% less sick days, 76% more engaged, and 40% less burnout. The science keeps demonstrating what is needed from leaders in order to make more productive organizations with well-being of the workforce being paramount. This is not about being "touchy-feeling" or "soft-skills" as some have referred to interpersonal skills, but of being focused on the human interactions of the workforce. If anything, they are about "hard-skills" since there so many areas for growth in this area and something that is crucial for the success of leaders and their workforce.

The above is part of the reason why the field of neuroscience and neuroleadership is growing. Because the more we learn about our brain at work and through our life experiences, the better we can equip leaders and their workers. In addition, as mentioned earlier as a leader you play a quasi-psychologist, sociologist, and anthropologist. This has led to the growth and extensive writing and research in this area. The concept of NeuroLeadership coined by David Rock, focuses on how individuals make decisions, problem-solving, regulating emotions, collaborating, and influencing others, while facilitating change in a social environment (Rock & Ringleb, 2013). Neuroscientists tell us that the primary role of the brain is to survive and that our brain is wired to be on the lookout for threat or stress. This survival mechanism is running more in the subconscious. We don't get up in the morning consciously thinking I have to survive today, but subconsciously our brains do. This is where you, Ms. or Mr. Boss, in your role as a leader becomes increasingly important.

Considering that those of you in a managerial role are under immense pressure and stress due to all of the demands that they have, it is important to recognize how our brain can help or hinder us. It already has been noted in the book, *Dying for a Paycheck* that stress makes work the fifth cause of death. It has also been highlighted that a manager's emotion are contagious and has a bigger impact on their worker's health than their doctor. Which means it all begins with you in a leadership role.

For these reasons and the ones cited earlier on the changing psychology of the workforce, it is imperative for leaders learn to monitor and maximize the strength of their brain in order to create an organizational environment that will be conducive to minimizing threat and stress in their workers. We've learned that what our brains need is a leader to create environments that feel safe and certain. That we need leaders who communicate well, make understanding them easy, create fair and transparent processes, so our brains do not waste precious effort in second guessing or trying to understand what to do next (Swart et al., 2015). Bottom line, what neuroscientists have found that when we humans are stressed, frustrated, or angry, we literally get dumbed down.

For this reasons and you might want to ask yourself, are you taking care of what you are feeding your brain? Are you monitoring how you react to situations? As you reflect on yourself consider are you an effective communicator? Are you listening to understand and not to respond? Are you demonstrating empathy? Do you create a safe and transparent environment? Are you minimizing situations where the workforce might have to second-guess what you really mean when you are communicating an expectation?

From neuroscience or as some refer to it neuropsychology this is further reinforced as we've learned that "the power of human connection is wired into our brain through evolution and socialized into our mind" (Swavely, 2024a). This is increasingly important particularly as technology continues to grow, organizations continue to adapt and change, and today's worker psychology continues to evolve. This is even more important when more are working remote or hybrid, globalization continues to grow and in turn can make it more difficult (if we allow it) to connect.

As mentioned earlier, those in a managerial capacity are always on as their teams, colleagues, and even organization (depending on their level) are watching what they say, don't say, do, and don't do. In other words, are you really modeling what you preach? And a contributing part to helping your team is to be somewhat of an inspiration. Dr. Swavely in one of his blogs highlighted the following: "Inspirational leadership is the art and science of creating an environment that activates the emotional centers of the follower's brain to achieve results important to the organization" (Swavely, 2024b).

This gets at a key component of your role as the boss, of ensuring you're tapping into your team's brain in a positive way. That you're also aware that we all have biases, and they can get in the way of being an effective leader. Most don't like to admit that we have biases, but it has been found that 75% of executives have witnessed favoritism in hiring, have found that 94% of policies intended to minimize favoritism were ineffective, and that 83% found that favoritism produced poor-quality promotion decisions (Hamel & Zanani, 2020). It is estimated that we have about 150 biases, many for our survival. But what we have to be cautious about is when an unconscious bias might get in the way of creating an inclusive environment for our whole team, irrespective of their diverse background. When without meaning to, we might prefer one staff member over another, in other words have our favorites-something most in management don't like to admit.

To possibly help in this area, empathy is growing as an important competency for leaders. When a leader demonstrates empathy, they are basically letting their employee know that they understand their situation. Research has found that leaders who demonstrate empathy led to improved performance (Goleman & Boyatzis, 2019). Being empathetic and a leader's emotions has been shown to impact a group's psychology and sociological experience or their workplace experience and in turn their engagement.

It has been found that leaders who elicit laughter tend to outperform those that did not, in other words their emotions are contagious (Glaser & Glaser, 2019). This is further supported by research highlighting the importance of brain chemistry. For example, when a leader criticizes an employee or they feel rejected their body produces cortisol, a hormone in our brain that activates conflict aversion. On the other side, positive comments by a leader elicit oxytocin, a hormone that increases communications, collaborations, and trust.

As mentioned previously our brain's primary purpose is to survive, to protect us from danger (Mosley & Irvine, 2021). One way to consider helping your team maintain a positive mindset and minimize the survival mentality is to create an environment of gratitude and appreciation. Appreciating your staff is an inexpensive and value-add gesture for all in leadership roles to remember and maximize. And while some of you reading this might think we know this, know that many don't seem to or at a minimum don't seem to demonstrate this through their behaviors. As was highlighted in the Ted Talk 2030 Workforce Crisis mentioned earlier, where appreciation came out as the number one thing over 200,000 worldwide were looking for in their next employer. Obviously they were not getting this in their current employer.

For those in a leadership role as you interact with others, this interaction brings their and your psychology to the exchange. They and you bring into the interaction how you feel about the situation, how you feel about each other, and any other issues that may be lingering in our minds. Not only this, but you also create team dynamics and a departmental or organizational culture based on your beliefs and in turn behaviors. In essence, as mentioned earlier you play a key role in the sociology of your group and also create an organizational or team environment or culture by how you behave and how you treat your workforce.

This is particularly important when it is estimated that organizations spend $300 billion on health care costs and absenteeism due to work stress (Platt, 2020). And as it was noted earlier you the leader play more of an important role on your workers health than their doctors. It has been found that 55% of workers were stressed due to workplace changes and stress has also been found to impact turnover. Reducing stress and creating a workplace where the workers feel connected can positively impact engagement and reduce turnover by almost 60% (Aldrich, 2016). This alone should lead you as a leader to ensure you're creating a healthy workplace where everyone can feel engaged, safe, understood, and productive. Leadership is all about relationships and building connections which is how we are neurologically wired.

Some of the previous mentioned stress comes from having too many things to do in a short amount of time. This has led to many trying to multitask. In reality, multi-tasking is a created term for something we really don't do. What our brain actually does is switch-task, or switch between two tasks very quickly and not very effectively. What we don't realize is that so-called multitasking (or switch-tasking) has been found to negatively affect our productivity, memory, lowers IQ, and can be addicting (Klemm, 2016). We need to realize that when we multitask or switch-task as leaders we tend to minimize our effectiveness and those with our teams and workforce.

What makes this worse is the number of meetings taking place usually back-to-back. This has been shown through research that what our brain needs are breaks (Work Trend Index Special Report, 2021). This research found breaks actually improve our ability to focus during meetings. How not only creating an organizational environment and culture where having breaks between meetings is not only allowed but welcomed by management, and that those in a leadership role actually model what they are expecting. Some organizations have actually set up a day of the week as "no meetings" day.

Some are using the technology to help them with this philosophy and prac-tice. They are looking to innovate and use technology to help build breaks into the worker's day. What do you as a leader do? How many back-to-back meetings are you in? How about your workforce? How can you help change this mindset and practice? How do you change the bias that more meetings lead to a more effective organization?

This of course has leadership and organizational implications. Remem-ber you have a bigger impact on your workforce that many in leadership role realize. Because of this there are those that have advocated for something that could guarantee leadership effectiveness. Some have written that this might be to have a leadership purpose—something bigger than the role or position (Swavely, 2020). The author points out that a well-designed lead-ership purpose comes from understanding ourselves, which includes our beliefs, values, emotions, and behaviors. He goes on to make the point that when leadership purpose is front and center there are three neurological chemicals engaged in our brain. The three are dopamine—which creates sensation of excitement and insight, serotonin—that creates of relief and accomplishment, and oxytocin—that creates sensations of trust and rela-tionship bonding.

As you can imagine all of these are needed when working in a fast-paced work environment. Leadership purpose might be key ingredient that those in a leadership role might truly want to consider. This in a time, where pur-pose has become a key component that the workforce is looking for and because of this some organizations have created a Chief Purpose Officer position.

This brings us to the point that learning to effectively use your brain in your daily interactions with others and recognizing how our brains are wired is a beginning. In the book, *The Mind of the Leader*, the authors highlight several techniques to consider including learning and practicing mindful-ness which has been shown to help monitor stress, clarity, and approaches to dealing with others.

Reflections from the workplace…

"I worked for a boss who showed favoritism and had an ego."—Hayley Miller

---

The Pre-fontal Cortex (PFC) is the executive function of our brain and is the part of the brain that works efficiently. This is part of brain that helps us deal collaboratively, critically analyze situations, and even serve as our breaks to stop us from saying or doing anything inappropriate when making decisions and under duress or stress. This is the part of the brain primarily at use when we are not under stress, threat, or feel frustrated.

Another area that impacts the PFC is our need to rest or sleep or unfortunately the lack of it. In several of his books, Dr. Medina highlights the need for sleep in his books "Brain rules for Aging," "The 12 Brain Rules," and "Brain rules for work." Some organizations like Apple, Microsoft, and other tech companies realize this and have introduced sleep pods in their workspaces. On a personal note, just remember the last time you did not get a good night's sleep, did you feel lethargic, slow, or irritable the next day? That's how most have described themselves when I have asked in the past. While you may not have sleep pods in your workspaces, what sort of environment are you creating so that your staff does not take their workplace worries home and not get a good night's sleep? The better they and you sleep, the more productive, effective, and engaging everyone will be.

Fortunately for us there is some research highlighting that the brain is capable of neuroplasticity or the ability to change itself, in other words you can learn to be a leader (Swart et al., 2015). These authors go on to highlight that when we're not under stress, the PFC is in control and primarily responsible for the higher-level executive functions for all of us. In other words, the PFC handles functions like self-control, complex problem solving, attention, memory among others. The PFC serves as the CEO of our brain when we're not under stress or duress.

Knowing this and knowing that our emotions are contagious, hence the term emotional contagion, as leaders you are in a prime position to remember that you bring to the workplace your psychological state. The better you can manage this as a leader, in other words manage your emotional intelligence, and not only be aware of your emotions but of those around you, the more effective you can be as a leader and in turn create a positive workplace experience for your team and workforce.

In his book, *Brain rules for Work*, Dr. Medina (2014) points out that leaders carry power by their position. However, this power is like heat, it can cook or burn a meal. Hence, you in a leadership role are in a position to create a great place to work or a dysfunctional work environment, depending on how your mindset and behavior. This is particularly important to keep in mind when what the research tells us is that the workforce is looking for leaders who give them meaning and value them (Swart et al., 2015).

Dr. Medina also points out that we only have one brain, for both work and life and that we should manage it in a positive manner. This further highlights the need for leaders and organizations to create a great workplace experience by enabling a work-life integration, which supports their team members to take time away from work. In addition, leaders need to listen, to truly listen. To listen not to respond but to understand. As the authors in *The Mind of the Leader* found, that only 8% of leaders are effective listeners and communicators.

Reflections from the workplace...

"I had someone who listened and cared. He treated me fair and trusted me with my responsibilities and mentored me. He even gave me advise for career development."

In addition, since the brain's primary role is to survive, it is incumbent on leaders to create a safe workplace environment by ensuring employees feel there is psychological safety. By psychological safety, Amy Edmundson from Harvard has equated psychological safety to oxygen. We don't notice it when we have it but know when it is missing. By this, workers need leaders who will create a workplace environment that makes them comfortable to raise a minority or different view of issues while not feeling threatened by raising the diverse point of view.

There are some brain-related issues that we need to educate and help develop our leaders and workforce on. One such issue is self-regulation, a brain-based capacity that influences work-place productivity by relying on our self-awareness and ability to manage how we think, feel, and proactively create positive thoughts and feelings.

Another one is mindfulness, that is considered not a "nice to have," but a necessity for those in leadership. Mindfulness has been found to affect perception, body awareness, pain tolerance, emotion regulation, introspection, complex thinking, and sense of self (Congleton et al., 2019). In summary, mindfulness and other mental techniques like compassionate meditation, transcendental meditation, are just some of the useful tools that leaders can use to regulate emotions (Swart et al., 2015).

These areas support from a brain's perspective, what the workers of today need from a psychological perspective and what they are expecting from their organizations and leaders. As mentioned earlier, today's workforce is looking for happiness, purpose, and in turn a great workplace experience so that they can be more engaged, have a more positive experience in their workplace which in turn leads to improved productivity.

Our brains are also wired to look for certainty. This is why when an organization and in turn a leader is driving change, they need to address the "why" for the change, so the workers brain is clear on the change. To do this leaders will need to be clear in their communications and expectations (Swart et al., 2015), as the quote says at the beginning of this chapter. Addressing the why can in turn minimize uncertainty and stress and engage the workforce sooner so they can help enable the organizational change.

Leaders will need to be self-aware of ensuring a positive mindset and in turn minimizing stress so as to be increasingly effective and more productive. Leaders also need to become aware of any behaviors getting in their way of effective leadership and work on them. The neuroscience field has recognized that it takes on average two months to forge a new habit (Minks, 2024). What behavior are you trying to make a habit as you continue to grow in your leadership effectiveness? Are you focusing on them and are you getting some assistance from someone such as an Executive Coaching, your manager, a colleague, a mentor, and your team?

The great breakthrough in neuroscience is about our brain's neuroplasticity. Believing you can do something, such as being an effective leader, for the brain it is as if you are an effective leader. Your neural pathways reshape themselves based on what you're telling yourself (Hollins, 2019). In other words, if you start believing you are an effective leader and try to work on areas to focus and improve on, you'll be on the beginning of personal journey of change for you and those that work with you.

Amy Cuddy highlighted a variation of this in her Ted Talk about the power of our body language has on our brain (Cuddy, 2012). And while this may be helpful, it is also important that we ensure you're getting a comprehensive view on your effectiveness and that it is not just your perspective.

Bottom line, your workers need to feel (yes feel) and believe that they are in a good workplace and that their leaders, their boss, you have their best interest at heart by creating a safe, brain-friendly, happy, and psychologically safe workplace. That you as a leader are creating a place where they have autonomy since I have not met anyone that wants to be micro-managed, purpose, doing work that is bigger than them, and having the opportunity for personal mastery, to continue to learn and develop irrespective of age, role, etc. Ensuring as a leader you are creating a positive workplace starts with being self-aware (Swavely, 2023). Being self-aware is the first step to ensuring that you're trying to create a workplace where workers are productive, and in turn lead to overall organizational effectiveness, which is after all why you were placed in the boss role ☺.

Summary

> *Reflections from the workplace…*
>
> *"I had a boss who basically indicated that he did not expect for me to work for him forever. However, while we worked together to do the best and enjoy our time together. He was very open when I was considering other opportunities outside of the organization and mentored me. He is still until today one of my best bosses I have ever worked for.*

Neuroscience and Neuroleadership continue to gain research and insights as further research, and books keep getting written about it. While fairly new to the concept of leadership, more research is highlighting its importance. Just like Emotional Intelligence gained prominence in the 20th century, these concepts are highlighting for leaders and their workplace the importance of what is going on inside our brains when dealing with each other, at work, and the implications of leadership. The growing importance of these concepts in the workplace, where humans work and cultures are created will continue to play a role with particular focus on leaders.

CHAPTER 6

CONSIDERATIONS: FROM "THE BOSS" TO LEADERS

ABSTRACT

This last chapter summarizes what is taking place in today's organizations and your role as a leader to effectively work through these issues with your teams. To create a healthy work environment. And even more importantly to take care of yourself in the journey. Because effective leadership is not a destination but a journey. To reflect and focus on delivering on the organizational objectives by developing, enabling, and empowering your teams and workforce. The most valuable resource you have is your workforce. Look to behave as if you truly believe this and want to do right. As you read this final chapter, consider your progress. Consider checking with your teams and workforce. Following this chapter are a few questionnaires to consider using as part of your journey.

Keywords: Leadership; human intelligent workplace; human centered workplace environment; worker psychology; human capital trends; organizational environment

Richard Branson, CEO of Virgin Air and Virgen Records has been credited with saying "Respect is how you treat everyone, not just those you want to impress." This is something that the former co-founder and CEO of Southwest Airlines Herb Kelleher also believed in, and it is hard to argue with Southwest's success under his leadership at the time that this might not be good advice, especially for front line leaders. So how you take care of your employees and team members who in turn service the client might make the difference between success and failure.

The BOSS for 21st Century Organizations, pages 61–75
Copyright © 2026 by Emerald Publishing Limited
All rights of reproduction in any form reserved.
doi:10.1108/978-1-80592-158-520251008

At the core of these beliefs is what leaders need to do to enable and create a more human-centered organization. It is also about appreciation, something that workers are looking for from their leaders in their workplace beyond a paycheck. To ensure that their leaders are empowering, motivating, engaging, and creating a great workplace experience for them.

The following article highlighted the key traits needed by managers today. The Young Entrepreneur Council (YEC) highlighted 13 essential traits for great leadership (YEC, 2024). Some of the traits consisted of empathy, transparency, listening skills, ability to adapt, a desire to learn, and problem-solving skills among others. This is further supported by an article that highlighted what differentiates good leaders from bad managers.

The good leaders are accessible, recognize their worker's concerns, follow through while providing their team the bigger picture of situations and decisions, and keep lines of communication open (Schwantes, 2024a). Another study points out that in the next 5 years some of the skills needed will be leadership and influence, motivation, critical thinking, and systems thinking among others (Taylor, 2024).

Others go on to point out that among other things that effective leaders have in common is that they trust their employees, view their employees as people first, and communicate and try to be honest among others (Davis, 2024). All of these studies and research continue to point out that ultimately the interpersonal skills will be foundational and an imperative, particularly for those in a leadership role.

In addition, trust, a concept that has been written and discussed extensively as a requirement for effective leadership continues in the forefront. With all of the changes needed to be addressed by organizations and its leadership, trust has become something that leaders need to create and ensure others trust them, because it also has business implications (Ho, 2021). The situation that sometimes occurs unfortunately is that those in a leadership role might inadvertently diminish trust while not intending to. This can be done by not being clear in what they are communicating and expecting, by not listening, by not walking their talk or modeling what they are expecting (Ferrer, 2024).

Listening, which most tend to believe to do well, but unfortunately not well enough, can impact a leader's performance by up to 40% (Bradberry, 2024). And as the author goes on to point out, listen also spells "silent." He highlights that good listeners focus, put away their phone (unfortunate that we have to say this one), ask good questions, practice reflective listening, and don't pass judgment among others. In other words, they listen to understand and not to respond and don't try to multitask or switch-task.

Something to consider is to truly reflect on what I have written above and ask yourself truly, how are you doing? Have you checked with others to confirm your own perception? Are your intentions aligning with your behaviors?

As Scott Cawood writes in his book *The New Work Exchange* urging organizations to put people first so that organizations can enable them to keep up with the changing expectations of their consumers. He goes on to point out what I've mentioned before that today's workforce is looking for organizations that care and support them and that organizational priorities are aligned with their expectations. Today's workforce is looking for greater influence, choice, and control. Todays' boss needs to lead people instead of employees (Cawood, 2023).

Reflections from the workplace…

"I worked for someone that when she gave me feedback for not doing something right, it was in a constructive manner, and I felt I had let her down and wanted to do better. She treated me with dignity, respect, and as an adult."

John Taylor, the President, and CEO of Society of Human Resources (SHRM) has said, "To shape the future work, leaders must be at the forefront of the evolving issues facing our workforce today." This means that those fortunate enough to be in a leadership role, need to recognize the changing expectations of today's workforce. They are not just working for a paycheck. While a paycheck is the fundamental reason for all to work, yet many studies continue to highlight that most are looking for more than just a paycheck. Which is why 200,000 individuals globally were looking for appreciation in their next employer. Some of the organizations that continue to highlight these changes through research are Gallup, Conference Board, Pew Research, and others.

As mentioned earlier, today's workers are looking for purpose, mastery, appreciation. They are also looking for happiness, a great workplace experience, and to be listened to. They are looking for a boss who is empathetic and understands their concerns and perspectives, is compassionate, and treats them not as just an employee, but a human being trying to make a living and a difference.

In addition, some other considerations to make as you evaluate how effective you are doing as a leader is to stop, pause, and reflect on what might be your leadership purpose. Why did you step into this role? What drives you? How truly self-aware are you on how you may be impacting your team? Are you making work meaningful, letting your people shine, leading from the heart, meeting the needs of your team, and sharing your power (Schwantes, 2024b)?

There are a serious of additional questions to consider as a leader that highlights that if you can answer them in the affirmative then you might be making them part of your leadership behaviors and in turn you might be a better leader than you think. For example, with so much organizational change taking place, how effective are you at managing transitions? How well do you take ownership for your leadership responsibilities? How well do you handle conflict? Because this will occur. Last, how well do you handle people and personalities? These are important to keep in mind as they have been identified as the superpowers that every manager needs (Lofranco, 2021).

This further highlights the importance of maintaining a healthy and well-being work environment that comes from a positive organizational culture (Seppala & Cameron, 2015). This is done by fostering connections, demonstrating empathy, helping others as needed, encouraging open dialog. This can only happen when you as the leader highlight the importance of this for you and demonstrate through your behaviors that you support it, and in turn positively impact the organizational culture.

All of this is taking place in a workplace that can now more than before even include a remote workforce. And this remote, hybrid workforce, along with their colleagues that are actually present in the workplace are looking to remain engaged. This is important to keep in mind since there is contradictory information on the topic of a remote or hybrid workplace. In some instances, managers have considered those in the office to be more productive or promotable (Morgan, 2021). While other work points to remote workers being 72 minutes more productive (Daly, 2023). Possibly because not having to travel into work, may allow for the workers to work versus travel into workplace.

This further highlights the biases that those in management can have. As the saying goes, "out of sight of mind." Some of the thoughts and questions to consider here are the following. Are people in the office really more productive or does our distance bias have something to do with this? In addition, as I've read in some LinkedIn postings, when the argument is made about organizational culture and having people return to the office (RTO) after the pandemic, the counter to this is that organizational culture was never about a building. Last, the question remains if we could be productive during the Pandemic, why can't we after the Pandemic?

And while there may be much debate on whether RTO or remote/hybrid is better, some recent research highlights offices were not being used as much as claimed prior to the pandemic (Elliott, 2025). It seems that only 50%–65% offices were utilized pre-pandemic. Some organizations like Atlassian and Airbnb among others are taking a more progressive approach and not abandoning remote and hybrid work setups.

In reality, those in management can positively impact a remote and hybrid workplace if they really want to. But it will take a shift in mindset, to challenge our own biases, and a behavior change in order to be successful. As a leader of a remote or hybrid workplace, you'll need to make the time to stay in touch via technology and maintain the human touch utilizing technology as a tool and not an excuse. It will also take organizational support, accountability, and a reinforcement framework for leaders to be an effective virtual leader.

Another way to consider it, is based on the following model in Figure 6.1 which is a visualization of an organizational environment where leaders manage in a remote/hybrid/virtual and co-located organizational setup. A visualization of the organizational benefits when done correctly and the flow from leader behaviors to employee satisfaction, engagement, and happiness which can then position the organization

Figure 6.1

Leader-Employee Relationships in a Virtual/Remote/Hybrid & Co-located Workplace.

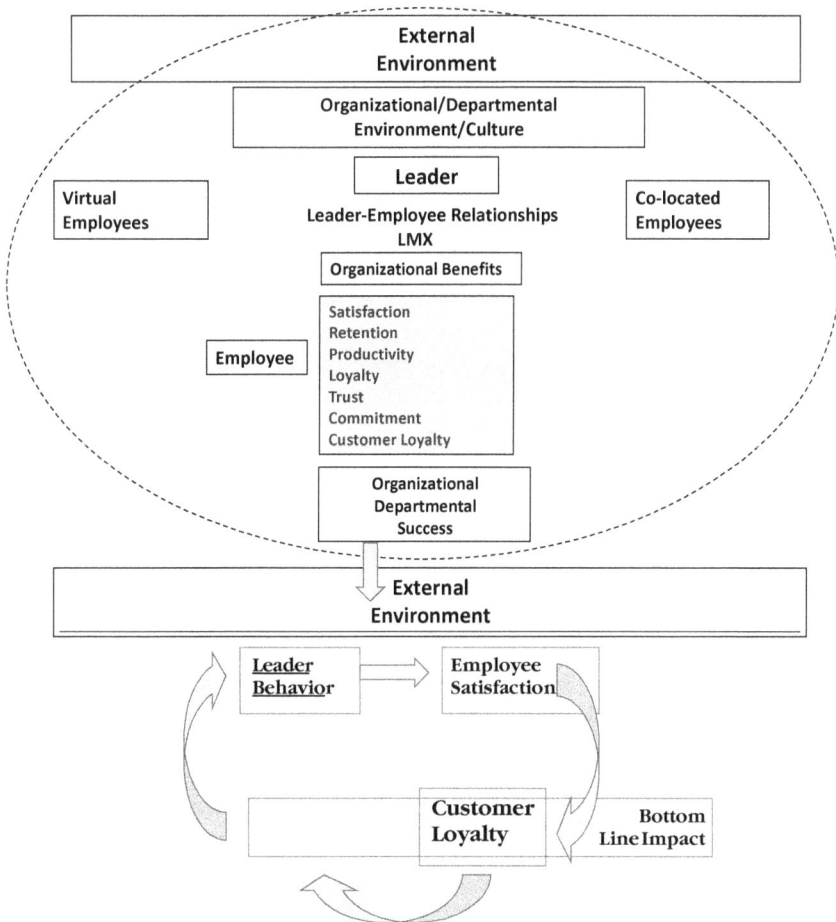

Source: Author's own.

for customer loyalty. The model highlights the wholistic and systemic approach needed with the benefits when supported correctly. It is also a model created based on my.

Up to now you've read about the state of work and how societal and organizational factors are impacting and will continue to impact organizations and work. Expectations of how your subordinates expect to be treated are changing among workers, especially Millennials. This is highlighted and reinforced in a Harvard Business Review article republished after it was written over a decade ago by Peter Drucker titled "They're not employees, they're people" (Drucker, 2002).

Drucker goes on to emphasize the importance of employee relations and how this is not something organizations or management want to offload or take lightly. And this was almost 20 years before the Pandemic, which has turned everything on its head. Where now we have terms like quiet quitting or quiet hiring, unemployment is at all-time lows, there are skill shortages, aging and growing diverse society, and organizations are competing more than ever for talent.

The most admired organizations in the world recognize agility, authenticity, emotional intelligence, diversity, working collaboratively, and having a global mindset will be crucial for the success of any organization in the 21st century (Royal & Stark, 2016). These organizations realize that effective leadership will be crucial in order to attract, develop, and retain a quality workforce. While technology continues to evolve at dramatic speed and sometimes overwhelm organizations and its employees the very important roles for the 21st century will be empathy, collaboration, creating, leading, and developing relationships (Colvin, 2015). These are all people skills that you as a boss will need to model and "walk the talk" while also expecting your teams to demonstrate the same.

In their article "Getting ready for the jobs of the Future," the Boston Consulting Group (BCG) highlight that the skills needed for the future will be mindfulness, emotional self-regulation, growth, decisiveness, human-to-human, team-focused, and optimism among others (BCG, 2024). They go to point out that leaders will need to be on the lookout for collaborative opportunities, to prioritize lifelong learning, to emphasize a collaborative problem solving while creating a culture of dialog. Those of you in a leadership role reading this book have this opportunity and challenge in front of you. The research is pointing out what will be needed for tomorrow's workplace. Now it's up to you to make it a reality. Are you doing this already? If not what will it take? What can you specifically do to make the future workplace a more human-centered workplace? Is your organization ready or what will it need to do to get ready?

The role you will play as a leader at any level will have dramatic implications for your organization. While organizations have their organizational culture, department managers create their own departmental environment and their own brand. How you treat your subordinates will get around the organization as either being an effective or ineffective boss.

Some advice given in a previous article makes a lot of sense (Nip, 2016). The author highlights that recognizing you're not perfect and will make mistakes while remaining humble will be instrumental. In addition, listening has always been and will continue to be a crucial skill and practice that your subordinates will appreciate (just see some of the ineffective boss comments in the previous chapter). And last do not forget that you're not only a manager but a role model.

If you model some of the behaviors of the effective bosses shared previously, you have an opportunity to create a collaborative and engaged workforce and environment. This will also lead to a healthy workforce. This can be done by not only leading by example, but ensuring your team believes in a culture of collaborating, by maintaining an environment of transparency by maintaining open lines of communications, building a sense of community among your team and department, and ensuring there is ongoing development for all (Le Cren, 2016).

There is one point of view that forces are converging in ways that we may have not experienced before, and it will require a different mental paradigm for success going forward. There has been much change, and some would say turmoil from a social, economic, political, and environmental, further enabled with the pandemic and this positions organizations to adapt and change, because what got them here will not enable them to move to the future. Just like new business models exists today that did not in the 20th century. Organizations like Airbnb that do not own hotel rooms, or Uber that do not own taxes. These changes will continue.

Leaders need to understand that workers are expecting to bring more of themselves to work. To have more flexibility, autonomy, happiness, purpose, and overall great work experience and higher expectations of their leaders. That hybrid, remote, and flexible working scenarios are now expected, not just wished for. That what leaders need to consider is to work this collectively, instead of individually. Because as I engage with leaders in workshops and in team retreats, as they share their concerns, they find that they have more in common then they realize and in turn have an opportunity to work together for the good of all.

And that in order to improve as a leader, you will need to work on your interpersonal skills (or as some like to refer to them as the soft skills, interpersonal skills, or worse touch-feely). Because it has been pointed out that 85% of your leadership success will come from your soft-skills, such as emotional intelligence, communications, critical thinking, and others (Partaker, 2024). By the way, there is nothing really soft about them.

> *Reflections from the workplace…*
>
> *"I worked for someone that always yelled. He always walked into work in a bad mood, which made the rest of us nervous and also in a bad mood."—Lauren Diaz*

Others recommend that leaders need to focus on the three areas of concern which are the future of workers or the who, the future of working or the what, and the future of work or the why (Howard-Grenville & Empson, 2023). The Ted 2030 Workforce Crisis addresses one of the key things that employees were looking for in their next employer which was appreciation.

As you consider your role in the 21st century organizations, you must remember that you ultimately create the environment and departmental culture. What sort of culture you create is important to never lose sight of because culture can support the success of your departmental, functional, or organizational initiatives by attracting great talent, it can enable an engaging environment and motivated workforce, and set you and your team up for success (Brighton, 2016). Brighton goes on to point out that if you focus on your culture by being sure you're *clear* on behaviors that are expected, you hold everyone *accountable* to these expectations, you ensure there are effective leader-employee *relations*, and develop your team's *esteem* through recognition, you then focus on your departmental and organizational culture.

As Figure 6.2 highlights a study by the BCG, when 200,000 job seekers were asked what they were looking for in their next employer, number one was a "thank you." The top four are about organizational culture. Salary was, as you can see, number 8.

Another key and fundamental piece to keep in mind is the following. We have been focused on what the workforce is looking for and the new psychology of today's workforce. But one key contributor to all of this is about you as a leader. Remember emotional contagion that I mentioned earlier that your emotions are contagious. Jacob Morgan argues that is not only about the workforce, but really about you the leader (Morgan, 2024). He goes on to show different examples of CEOs and how they led their organizations to success or not. He puts the focus on you the leader. What are you modeling, what is your strategic direction?

This book is intended for a multi-varied audience, irrespective of level, it is for that one that is considering a leadership role, and it is for those that support leaders. In the end we want to ensure leaders are successful not only for them, but for their workforce and organizations. In organizations that have become bureaucratic, they tend to put the institution first, followed by the individual, that leads to output. But in organizations that evolve away from being bureaucratic to more humanistic or to Humanocracy as the authors refer to it, they tend to place the individual first, followed by the

Figure 6.2

Job Preferences of 200,000 Job Seekers.

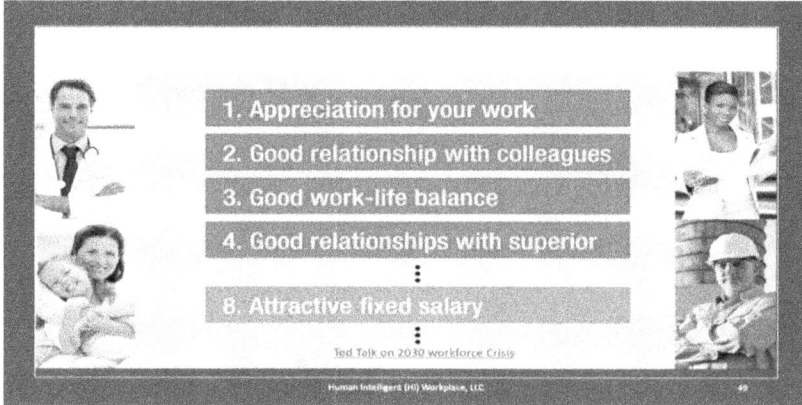

Source: Rainer Strack (2014).

organization, and then impact (Hamel & Zanini, 2020). What is the focus of your organization and in turn its leaders?

A few last pieces to keep in mind as a leader is about your role in change. Because once you stepped into the leader role you accepted the challenge of becoming an agent of change in your organization. One of the key roles you will play as a leader is influencing others through change. As you do this you should consider the Lippit-Knoster 5 Components of Organizational Change model (Lippit & Knoster, 1987). In this model the authors begin with the need for leadership commitment and support. Beyond these which are fundamental, they also include Vision, Skills, Incentive, Resources, Action Plan. All are needed but each brings a different problem when missing. If vision is missing you get confusion, when skills are missing you tend to get anxiety, when incentive is missing you get gradual change, when resources are missing you get frustration, and last when you're missing an action plan, you tend to get false starts. As highlighted by the authors each are needed and when one is missing it brings different implications to bear to make the change more difficult to implement.

The other important piece to keep in mind when it comes to change, and that is if you are taking care of yourself? Like the message that is given to you when you board a plane when it comes to air masks, put yours on first before you help others. The same is relevant here for you as a leader. In order for you to help and influence others through change, you need to ensure you're taking care of yourself. Some things to consider as you ensure you are healthy and effective is the following. Keeping in mind the neuroscience and neuroleadership chapter these following recommendations are important for you mentally and in turn for your effectiveness.

For starters are you providing yourself some brain time? By this I mean are you practicing mindfulness, meditation, or yoga to name a few. Research into anyone of these to see the benefits and how to practice it. There are You-tube videos, websites, books, and articles on the power of these in order to take care of yourself. Are you exercising in some form or fashion? By this I do not mean you have to train for a marathon or something as difficult. But are you giving your body (and in turn your brain) some time. Exercise, something as simple as walking for 20 minutes a day 3 times a week has been shown to be healthy for our brain and overall health. This has also been highlighted as an area where we get our best ideas when thinking about difficult issues at work or in life. Are you getting your sleep? I mentioned this earlier that a good night's sleep helps out clear our mind. The brain needs it and all you have to remember is how you felt the last time you did not get a good night's sleep.

There are some others to consider. Do you listen to music? You read it right. It turns out our brain is melodic which is why we can remember where we were the last time we heard a particular song. It turns out certain type of music is not only good for our mental health, but also for our creativity. If you like music you may want to look further as to how it might help you as a leader. How about what do you eat? Yes you read right. There are actually a few documentaries on what we eat not only affects our health but also our mental health. There are actually numerous articles that highlight how certain foods affect our brain. How are your relationships? It turns out that in the Ted Talk of 2030 Workforce Crisis, when they asked participants what they were looking for in their next employer, relationships with my boss and my colleagues came out in the top four areas of priority. It has also been cited as a key to livelihood along with what you eat in the Blue Zones, those areas of the world where there are larger concentrations of centurions or those over 100. So, creating and maintaining healthy relationships will be important in the workplace and a key competency for leaders in 21st century organizations.

Last, are you having fun at work? Are you creating an environment of fun in the workplace? Research has shown that places where people believe they can be themselves and are having fun and be happy tends to create a psychologically safe environment and in turn more productive and effective organizations. What are you doing to make this a reality as a human first and leader second?

Hopefully you've learned through this book that an effective boss can increase productivity by helping their team members learn and grow and while creating an environment of creativity and innovation. This is something that all organizations will need to have in order to succeed in this VUCA or BANI environment, while being cognizant of the fact that their team members might make mistakes when trying to be creative and innovative (Aldrich, 2016). Aldrich goes on to point that good bosses are vision setters, results drivers, and goal guiders. In other words, they ensure alignment through development and growth of their team.

Effective leaders know that they don't become successful in a vacuum and by themselves. What they've recognized is that they've had someone that impacted them along the way, had a significant event that they never forgot, and last they were in an environment in their past that made them who they are today (Swain, 2016). For some the secret to being a good boss is through candor by providing guidance to their staff so that they position them for success (Lee, 2015). While I agree with candor I would suggest that an effective boss does this with caution, authencity, and in a genuine and helping way. Because remember the brain's primary role is to survive and when someone is approached about a mistake they made or offered "feedback," most get defensive.

By listening and being empathetic when working with your staff can lead to higher performance, by coaching, and engaging your team (Siner et al., 2016). A truly engaged workforce and team is enabled by establishing trust within your department and organization because unfortunately still today almost one third of workers don't trust their employers (Hogan, 2016). This can be done by being empathetic, resilient, and humble among other things. In addition, trust can be improved in the workplace, if you are transparent, communicate, and over-communicate, and by encouraging community among your team (Hart, 2016).

Reflections from the workplace…

"I worked for someone that did not trust the team and was constantly questioning actions which in turn led to everyone's demotivation and low team morale. He also micro-managed us."—Viena Perez

---

What you might want to ask yourself is what type of leader do you want to be? A good one or a great one? The great leaders look to truly engage and galvanize the workforce toward the vision and mission of the organization (Bailey, 2016). It is not that a good leader is necessarily bad, but it may not be enough. Great leaders inspire, motivate, and energize the team to greatness. Because it seems that we're even in a short supply of good leaders, never mind great ones.

In addition to this, great leaders know when and how to show they are human and express their emotions in a positive manner. This when over 90% of leaders try to suppress their emotions (Samples, 2024). And while I've mentioned before that our emotions are contagious, leaders need to know when and how to show their emotions. In other words, they need to demonstrate emotional intelligence. So, while we've been discussing here the behaviors of smart supervisors, ask yourself what will it take to truly engage your team to a higher level of excellence? What will you need to do?

In the book, Human Work, the author highlights the evolution and differences we can expect going forward. In the industrial economy, workers were seen as hired hands, in the knowledge economy, workers were seen as hired heads. For the human economy and for human-centered organizations, they will hire for hearts (Merisotis, 2020). As mentioned earlier, the workforce expectations have been changing and the Pandemic created a tipping point. This is why leaders now more than ever will need to manage the business and lead the workforce.

What you have stepped up to do now is to be a boss and hopefully an effective one. Here you've seen anecdotal comments of individuals that have worked for some that have been effective and ineffective bosses. You've also learned that there are dramatic changes taking place across the globe, in society, and in turn in the workplace. The worker of the 21st century especially the growing millennials have different expectations from their organizations and management team.

The SHRM President & CEO of the Society of Human Resources (SHRM) who as an organization that supports and provides development for Human Resources (HR) professionals has written and spoken extensively about these issues. He represents those professionals that partner with leaders and their workforce to provide HR policies and enable the creation of workforce friendly organizations. He makes the point that one of the biggest challenges going forward for organizations and its leaders is finding, hiring, and engaging the right talent (Taylor, 2021). As you look at these, and all issues highlighted in this book, ask yourself if you and your organization are ready? Would your workforce say you are?

Summary

This last chapter looked to highlight what is taking place in today's organizations and your role as a leader to effectively work through these issues with your teams. It looked to address what it will take to create a healthy work environment. And even more importantly to take care of yourself in the journey. Because effective leadership is not a destination but a journey.

To reflect and focus on delivering on the organizational objectives by developing, enabling, and empowering your teams and workforce. The most valuable resource you have is your workforce. Look to behave as if you truly believe this and want to do right.

As we begin to come to the end of the book, I suggest you consider the following as you continue in your journey to be a better boss by being a great leader.

LEADERS

LEADERS stands for the following:

Listen & **L**earn—this will be something you will need to demonstrate if you truly want the most out of your team. Leadership has been aligned with life-long learning. Continuing to learn and enabling your team to learn will be crucial to your success. When it comes to listening, in a study as highlighted in the book, *The Mind of the Leader*, they found that 8% of leaders were effective listeners and communicators. Listening to understand and not to respond will be crucial for leaders moving forward.

Engagement and **E**mpathy leads to a positive **E**xperience—engaging all by creating a transparent and a psychologically safe environment can lead to a positive workplace experience. Engaging the workforce has been found to lead to increased productivity, reduced turnover, and positive bottom-line implications. As mentioned before, today's workforce is looking for happiness, purpose, to be appreciated, and an empathic and compassionate leader who listens. This can lead to a positive workplace experience that today's workforce is looking for.

Accountability—if organizations are going to spend and invest in the millions for their leadership development, then they should hold those trained accountable for the behaviors they've been trained on. Whether this include 360 feedback, performance incentive plans, and/or any other combination, leaders should know how they are performing as leaders.

Diversity, **D**evelopment (Mastery) & Inclusion as an advantage. Maximizing the diversity your workforce and teams will be an imperative going forward, especially as the workforce continues to grow more diverse. And it will be particularly important, as increasing research continues to come out on the positive bottom-line implications of diversity. Ensuring that everyone feels included will be a growing imperative for the benefits of organizations. Diversity, Equity, and

Inclusion is not about including some at the expense of others. It is about leadership. Are you as a leader tapping into the diverse perspectives and strengths of your growing diverse workforce?

Environment (aka Departmental/Organizational Culture) should be something as a leader that you create with your team and enable them to make real. Remember, your attitude is contagious. So, make it a good one so your team members carry it forward to your clients and customers. Consider organizations that have made this an imperative like Publix and others.

Recognition and **R**espect should be part of your mantra and what you model. Establishing this behavior as core to your department and team will only help you and your team in achieving success in a positive manner. How you treat your staff is how they will treat each other and their customers. Recognition through appreciation turns out to be the number one thing that people were looking for in their future employer in a study of 200,000 participants worldwide per the Ted Talk, 2030 Workforce Crisis. In this study, pay was number 8, while relationship with the boss, colleagues, work-life integration, and number one was appreciation. In other words, a simple thank you can go far.

Systems Approach is all about considering a variety of aspects within the organization. Some of the considerations are organizational climate/culture, organizational values and how they are modeled, HR policies and practices, rewarding and accountability mechanisms (remember what gets measured gets done), and leadership and workforce expectations. Ensure that your organization is taking a wholistic approach to trying to become a more human, workforce focused organization that in turn will lead to the bottom line implications.

LEADERS is what you all need to try to live up to. Learn or relearn what it is to be an effective boss and how to demonstrate leadership. It is not a destination but a journey. Every day will be a learning experience, live it to the maximum, and work to make your job environment for you and others a great place to work.

While BoSS was meant as acronym and hook for this book, it has more times than not had a negative connotation. I am hoping this book will help you make it become a positive term. Maybe the following visual can serve as a good reminder on your journey. Will you be one of the ones to receive this message?

I'm reminded one way boss is translated into Spanish is "jefe." I had someone who use to work for me and always referred to me as "El Jefe" in what I interpreted to be with good intentions. As we parted ways as she moved on

Figure 6.3

Picture of a Signed Football Squeeze Signed by One of My Former Staff Members.

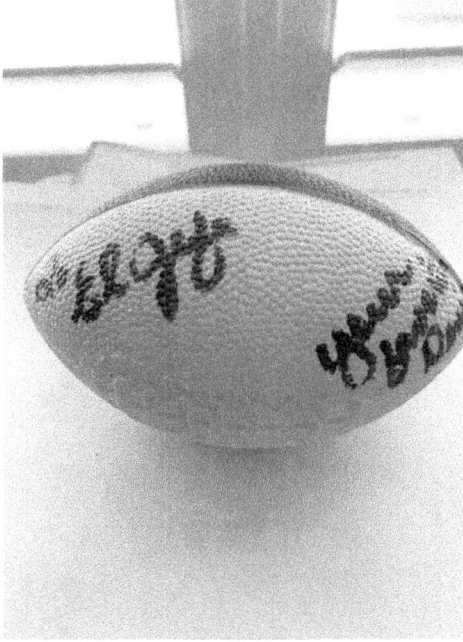

Source: Author's own.

to a new role, she had a small football that served as a stress relief squeeze toy on her desk. She signed it "El Jefe" and gave it to me with a smile and as a parting gift (see Figure 6.3). Until this day, I keep it on my bookshelf in my home office, as a reminder of the small gift but impact we can have on others in our leadership role through our actions and behaviors.

CHAPTER 7

CLOSING THOUGHTS

The above visual is a reminder for the reader of those that were our boss that made our workplace experience a positive one. Those that we would work for again. Those that treated us with respect, helped us grow, contribute, created a safe space at work for us to be relieved of stress from them, remember emotional contagion, and helped us to do our best.

My sincere intent, hope, and prayer is that you this book helped you truly reflect and reassess your leadership effectiveness. For your benefit and of your workforce, pausing along the way to reflect on how you may be behaving and how your good intentions may be landing and impacting others can only help.

We're usually going too fast at work and even life, to pause and reflect on how we're doing. As if, pausing might impact us negatively. Society is aging and I came across a piece of those older providing advice to the younger generations after them. A few mentioned was to stop, pause, and reflect. To enjoy the moment, whatever moment, because soon it will be part of the past. And I leave you with these thoughts. How are you doing as a boss/ leader? Have you checked this out with others? What will your legacy be after you've moved on? Take care of yourself and in turn take care of those entrusted in you to lead. I wish you the best and maybe, just maybe our paths will cross. If not, as Mr. Spock used to say, "Live long and prosper."

The BOSS for 21st Century Organizations, pages 77–79
Copyright © 2026 by Emerald Publishing Limited
All rights of reproduction in any form reserved.
doi:10.1108/978-1-80592-158-520251009

Some Questions to Consider...

I have been asking questions throughout the book. I had mentioned early and throughout for you to reflect on how you may be doing and how you may be coming across to those that work for you and with you. I wanted to at least capture some here for your consideration and as a reminder.

1. When it comes to the human capital trends that are impacting organizations, how ready is your organization? How ready are you?
2. Are you really capitalizing on the changing demographics in society and in turn in your organization?
3. Are you aware of your own biases? Are you open to others different than you, be this in age, demographic, or otherwise?
4. Do you have favorite team members? How is that landing with the rest of the team members? If you don't believe you have favorites, have you confirmed that others see it the way you do?
5. Are you in tune with the changing psychology of today's workforce? What are you doing about it?
6. Do you create a psychologically safe work environment? How do you know?
7. Do you understand how Artificial Intelligence may impact your organization and workforce today and in the future?
8. Are you enabling a human-centered organization by creating a human intelligent workplace? Is this needed from your point of view? Why or why not?
9. Are you taking care of yourself? How and when? Why or why not?
10. Are you ensuring others are taking care of themselves? How? Is it working for them? How do you know?
11. How effective are you at influencing change? How do you know? Are you clear on the why for change?
12. What is your purpose for being in a leadership role? Have you shared this with anyone to get someone else's reaction or perspective?
13. Have you thought about what your legacy might be?
14. Are you creating an environment or culture where people feel engaged, and their experience is a positive one?
15. How would others describe your leadership style? Why?
16. Have you ever spent time reflecting on how well you might be doing from a leadership perspective? When, why, or why not?
17. What do you believe might be your developmental areas? Would others agree with you, or would they have others?
18. How did this book help you on your leadership journey? Why or why not?

19. In your leadership experience, if there was something you could do again and differently, what would it be?
20. What would you advise to future leaders?
21. If you could go back, what would you advise to yourself as a younger and new supervisor?

APPENDIX: LANGAIPPE: EXTRA RESOURCES AND QUESTIONNAIRES

Lagniappe

Langiappe is a Spanish word that was frenchized (just invented this word-a blend of Spanish and French) and used quite a bit in New Orleans. It has been defined as a gift or a little extra. And so, having lived in New Orleans for several years, I follow suit in this book in providing you with a little extra. The extra are the following resources and questionnaires. Questionnaires intended to assist you in reflecting and possibly gaining insights from others in the following areas.

The two areas are: Human Intelligent (HI) Workplace, and Leadership Behavior Effectiveness (LBE). These two questionnaires are intended to provide you an opportunity to reflect on your organization and its practices when it comes to creating a more human-centered organization in today's changing workplace. The questionnaires are intended to provide you both a personal perspective along with workforce perspective, both from an organizational level and from your direct team's perspective (if you should decide to use as a 360-feedback loop). In summary, they are intended to help you and your organization helps itself.

They can also be found here and are available in Spanish if needed—https://humanintelligentworkplace.com/

Resources

(Note: The following questionnaires are also available in Spanish)

1. Human Intelligent (HI) Workplace Questionnaire
2. Leader Behavior Effectiveness (LBE) Questionnaire

Questionnaires

Human Intelligence (HI) Workplace Questionnaire

The HI instrument (see Figure A.1) can be used for you, your leadership team, and/or your respective department/functional team to assess how you are doing when it comes to enabling and creating an engaging workforce. It is an instrument for you to consider based on how HI workplace has been defined. To help you assess how humanly intelligent you believe your organization is. It is a questionnaire intended to help you reflect and provide your perception as to how you believe you and your organization are doing when it comes to issues like leadership, organizational culture, engagement, diversity, psychological safety, communications, collaboration, and workforce fulfillment.

Leader Behavior Effectiveness (LBE) Questionnaire

The LBE is for the reader who is in a leadership capacity to complete on themselves and also have an opportunity to gain insight from others in a

Figure A.1

Human Intelligent (HI) Workplace Model.

360-feedback manner, with insights, and input on your strengths and development areas from a managerial perspective.

Human Intelligent (HI) Workplace

Questionnaire

The following questionnaire is intended for the reader to assess from their perspective how well they believe their organization and leadership is creating a great workplace experience and environment where the workforce feels engaged while enjoying a positive workplace experience.

Human Intelligent (HI) Workplace Framework

HI Questionnaire

Human Intelligent (HI) Workplace Defined

Human Intelligent (HI) Workplace is defined as one where leaders model *effective* leadership behaviors by creating an organizational culture where the worker's *experience* is one of being engaged while *collaborating* with their diverse team members. It is a workplace where the workforce feels safe when raising different perspectives, taking risks, being innovative, or creative. It is a workplace where the workforce feels listened to and *understood* by their leaders. It is a workplace where the workforce finds *fulfillment* in the work they do and, in the organization, they work in.

The following describes each of the categories that I believe make a High Intelligent (HI) Workplace.

Leadership—effective leadership is fundamental to organizational success. It is one where an individual in a leadership position creates a positive workplace experience by focusing on the workforce in the organization.

i. **Why might this be important?** Effective leaders lead by positively influencing, engaging, and creating an inclusive environment where employees feel happy to work for the organization. Research has shown over the years that leadership has been defined as a role or a quality in a person, that may have a ripple effect on subordinates, department, and/or organization. Through their actions and behaviors, those in leadership position may positively or negatively impact their workers.

Organizational culture—Organizational Culture is all about shared values, attitudes, and practices that characterize an organization. It is the environment that the workforce is involved in and works in to deliver results.

i. **Why might this be important?** Organizational culture has been described as the personality of the organization. A healthy organizational culture has been associated with increased health of the workforce, engagement, increased retention, and overall productive organization. Leaders are instrumental in creating a positive organizational culture in order to ensure the workforce feels valued, listened to, engaged, fulfilled, psychologically safe, and motivated.

Engaged: Employee engagement is the **positive connection a person has with their work, work environment, leaders, and colleagues.** It's reflected in their attitude, effort, and involvement.

i. **Why might this be important**: Research has demonstrated that higher employee engagement positively influences organizational success. This has been associated with a workforce that is more vested in the outcomes. It has been found that when workers are engaged it leads to a positive worker experience creating an optimal environment for employees to do their work.

ii. Engagement is created by a positive employee experience which **has do with the people, systems, policies, and the physical and virtual workspace.** When it is positive, it can lead to a more engaged and productive workforce. This can lead to a more fulfilled workforce which is all about purpose and happiness. Today more and more of the workforce are looking for purpose in the work they do and want to be happy in the place they work in.

iii. Purpose has become increasingly important enough that some organizations are considering a Chief Purpose Officer at the C-suite level. A happy worker has become important enough where research has begun to show that a happy worker with a purpose is healthier, more intrinsically motivated, have higher job satisfaction, is less stressed, more productive, and can lead to lower attrition and an a more engaged workforce.

Diverse team—A diverse team is all about the <u>diversity of the workforce</u> along with ensuring all team members feel included and that they receive equitable opportunities to contribute. Diversity has been described as **any dimension that can be used to differentiate groups and people from one another.**

i. <u>**Why might this be important**</u>? Diversity is about empowering people by respecting and appreciating what makes them different, in terms of age, gender, ethnicity, religion, disability, sexual orientation, education, and national origin. When leaders and organizational culture support and take advantage of their diverse workforce, it leads to increased collaboration which is important for diversity and effective team dynamics.

ii. An effective team has been defined as a group of people with complimentary skills, committed to a common purpose, mutual goals, and well-defined working approach. Effective team members trust each other and hold themselves accountable.

Safe—This component is about <u>Psychological Safety</u>. Psychological safety in the workplace refers to the collective belief or acknowledgment that any member of the organization can voice their perspective and opinion (even if it is a minority point of view) without fear of punishment, exclusion, or humiliation.

i. **<u>Why might this be important?</u>** In a workplace that promotes psychological safety, employees are more likely to feel comfortable expressing their ideas and personalities, as there is a greater sense of trust and respect in the environment. In today's workplace where innovation and creativity can provide a competitive advantage, psychological safety will be important. In order to have an organization where innovation and creativity are valued, then you need an environment where risks and mistakes are accepted, and workers feel safe.

Listen—This is all about <u>communications</u> and how effective leaders are at communicating and listening to the concerns, ideas, and uniqueness of each of their team members. This is about how leaders listen, are empathetic, and compassionate when listening to their workers issues and concerns.

i. **<u>Why might this be important</u>**? Listening leads to learning. Communications and listening are imperative for leaders and their workforce's success. As busy as leaders are, when they listen to understand versus to respond it leads to a more engaged workforce. When leaders are empathetic and compassionate, this is driven by effective listening and communicating. Empathy has been defined as the capacity to understand or feel what another person is experiencing from within their frame of reference, that is, the capacity to place oneself in another's position.
ii. Everything mentioned above can help lead to a more fulfilled workforce.

Human Intelligent (HI) Workplace

Questionnaire

The following questionnaire is intended for the participant to assess from their perspective how well they believe their organization and leadership is creating a great workplace experience and environment where the workforce feels engaged while enjoying a positive workplace experience. We believe that organizational culture is a reflection of leadership.

The Human Intelligent (HI) workplace is defined as one in which leaders model effective *leadership* **behaviors** by creating an **organizational culture** in which the worker's experience is one of being **engaged** while collaborating *with the* various **members of their team**.

It's a workplace where the workforce feels **safe** to bring up different perspectives, take risks, be innovative or creative. It's a workplace where the workforce feels **heard** and understood by their leaders. It is a workplace where the workforce finds *satisfaction* in the work they do and, in the organization, in which they work.

Based on how HI is defined and explained, rate the following statements based on your perception, observations, and insights on your organization.

Scale: 1-Strongly Disagree (SD), 2-Disagree (D), 3-Neutral (N), 4-Agree (A), 5-Strongly agree (SA)

1. I believe our leaders demonstrate effective leadership by creating a positive workplace experience.

1	2	3	4	5
SD	D	N	A	SA

2. I believe our leaders support and create an environment where the workforce can challenge the status quo.

1	2	3	4	5
SD	D	N	A	SA

3. I believe our leaders support and maximize effective team dynamics.

1	2	3	4	5
SD	D	N	A	SA

4. I believe our organizational culture is a healthy one where employees can thrive and contribute.

1	2	3	4	5
SD	D	N	A	SA

5. I believe our organization has a collaborative work environment.

1	2	3	4	5
SD	D	N	A	SA

6. I believe our leaders support an environment where mistakes are accepted.

1	2	3	4	5
SD	D	N	A	SA

7. I believe the organizational experience for our workers is a positive one.

1	2	3	4	5
SD	D	N	A	SA

8. I believe our workforce is engaged because of how they are treated.

1	2	3	4	5
SD	D	N	A	SA

9. I believe our leaders demonstrate empathy when working with their teams and workforce.

1	2	3	4	5
SD	D	N	A	SA

10. I believe our leaders demonstrate effective communications and listening.

1	2	3	4	5
SD	D	N	A	SA

11. I believe our leaders serve as positive role models for a healthy organization.

1	2	3	4	5
SD	D	N	A	SA

12. I believe our leaders create a healthy organizational culture.

1	2	3	4	5
SD	D	N	A	SA

13. I believe our organizational culture is one that enables the work-force to be engaged.

1	2	3	4	5
SD	D	N	A	SA

14. I believe our leaders demonstrate compassion when working with their workforce.

1	2	3	4	5
SD	D	N	A	SA

15. I believe our organization has an environment where everyone can be innovative and creative.

1	2	3	4	5
SD	D	N	A	SA

16. I believe our workforce is committed due to a positive employee experience.

1	2	3	4	5
SD	D	N	A	SA

17. I believe our leaders through their actions and behaviors positively influence and engage their workforce.

1	2	3	4	5
SD	D	N	A	SA

18. I believe our leaders support an inclusive and diverse workforce and teams.

1	2	3	4	5
SD	D	N	A	SA

19. I believe our leaders enable an environment of trust and respect.

1	2	3	4	5
SD	D	N	A	SA

20. I believe our organizational culture supports being a HI Workplace.

1	2	3	4	5
SD	D	N	A	SA

Rating Insights

<u>17 questions</u> in the Agree and/or Strongly Agree lends itself to a more Human Intelligent (HI) Workplace. Consider what led you to this score. Revisit the ones that came out lower. Consider why this might be.

Thoughts on these scores—these scores present your organization as one that is more effective at being a Human Intelligent Workplace. What brought you to this conclusion? You might to check these out with others that took it and how they compare. Also now consider how do we keep this going? Look into the areas that perhaps were not as strong.

<u>13–16 questions</u> in the Agree and/or Strongly Agree lends itself to room for improvement in pursuing becoming a more Human Intelligent (HI) Workplace. Revisit the ones you rated as Agree or Strongly Agree and ensure you still agree with this rating. Pay particular attention to the ones you rated Disagree and/or Strongly Disagree. What led you to this rating? What should the organization do? What can you do?

Thoughts on these scores—these scores present that your organization is middle of the road or average. Consider finding out what your workforce or work team think. Look for ways to dig in deeper into the areas that are not so strong. Also visit those that you believe your organization or department is doing well. Validate these scores with others or have them take the instrument to compare with your scores.

<u>Less than 12 questions</u> in the Agree and/or Strongly Agree lends itself to deeper reflection on what is taking place in the organization and your perspective on it.

Thoughts on these scores—these scores show that your organization has some work to do based on your perception of the organization. Consider also checking these scores with others or have them complete the questionnaire. There is work to do here. Do not take it as a negative, but as a beginning to address and to develop a plan to help your organization become more humanely intelligent. You can also reach out to the HI Workplace organization for assistance.

Assess how you rated the following categories:

Leadership—questions 1, 11, 17, 19
Organizational Culture—questions 4, 12, 16, 20
Engagement—questions 7, 8, 13
Diversity and Teamwork—questions 3, 5,18
Psychological Safety—questions 2, 6, 15
Listening and Communications—questions 9, 10, 14

Demographics (Optional)

Gender:	Female___	Male___	No Choice___	
Age:	Below 30___	31–40___	41–50___	51 and older___
Tenure:	1 year or less___	1+ to 5 years___	5+ to 10 years___	10+ years___

Position in Organization

Executive___	Middle Manager___	First Line Supervisor___	Individual Contributor___

Considerations: If you're a leader, you should check your ratings with your respective team, department, or functional area (as appropriate). Assess how they differ with your perspective. Remember, that leader and workforce disconnect is a reality. You should also check to see how other demographics see the workplace. Once you and your staff or team have shared their perspective, you should model effective leader behaviors by engaging others in addressing the issues going forward and creating a path forward in ensuring you create an HI workplace on the journey to becoming a human-centered organization.

Other Considerations

If **Leadership** is higher than the other categories while initially appearing good, there might be a disconnect. If leadership drives culture, engagement, psychological safety, demonstrates listening and communications, and enhances diversity and teamwork, then how could they be lower? You may be experiencing the "we're ok" syndrome. This is when we leaders think they're being effective, but others need help.

If **<u>Organizational Culture</u>** is high and others are lower, you may want to assess how this can be? Because organizational culture is a summary and comprehensive view of all the other categories.

If **<u>Engagement</u>** is higher than others, while this is good if accurate, you'll want to assess how this this can be while the others are lower. You'll also want to assess how your team rates this category. This will inform you of further research as to why you and your team are seeing this category the way you do.

If **<u>Diversity and Teamwork</u>** are higher than others, you may want to find out how this is possible if other categories are lower. Find out what is happening here that you're rating higher than others. Also confirm how your scores compare with your team. If they are different, you'll want to understand why.

If **<u>Psychological Safety</u>** is higher than others this might be good. However, you'll want to assess how this can be higher, and the others be lower, since they are so dependent on each other. Additionally, you'll want to compare how your team rate this category and if there is a disconnect.

If **<u>Listening and Communications</u>** are higher than others this is good. But again, you'll need to compare with your team's ratings. Also you'll need to assess how this one can be higher, yet the others be lower. At initial glance it seems like this cannot be accurate when the other categories are low since leadership communications (or lack of it) has overall impact on the other categories.

More details

Each of the categories that make up a High Human Intelligence (HI) workplace is described below.

1. **<u>Leadership</u>**: <u>Effective leadership</u> is critical to organizational success. It is one in which a person in a leadership position creates a positive workplace experience by focusing on the organization's workforce.
   - **Why might this be important**? Effective leaders lead by positively influencing, engaging, and creating an inclusive environment where employees feel happy to work for the organization. Research has shown over the years that leadership has been defined as a role or quality in a person, which can have a ripple effect on subordinates, the department, and/or the organization. Through their actions and behaviors, those in leadership positions can have a positive or negative impact on their workers.

2. **<u>Organizational Culture</u>**—Organizational culture has to do with shared values, attitudes, and practices that characterize an organization. It's the environment in which the workforce is engaged and in which they work to get results.
   - **Why might this be important?** Organizational culture has been described as the personality of the organization. A healthy organizational culture has been associated with increased workforce health, engagement, increased retention, and overall productive organization. Leaders are critical to creating a positive organizational culture in order to ensure that the workforce feels valued, heard, engaged, fulfilled, psychologically safe, and motivated.

3. **<u>Engaged</u>:** Employee engagement is the **positive connection a person has with their work, their work environment, their leaders, and their colleagues.** It is reflected in their attitude, effort and involvement.
   - **Why it might be important**: Research has shown that higher employee engagement positively influences organizational success. This has been associated with a workforce that is more interested in outcomes. It has been found that when workers are engaged, a positive experience occurs for workers, creating an optimal environment for employees to do their jobs.
   - Engagement is created through a positive employee experience that **has to do with people, systems, policies, and the physical and virtual workspace.** When it's positive, it can lead to a more engaged and productive workforce. This can lead to a more satisfied workforce that is all about purpose and happiness. Today, more and more of the workforce is looking for purpose in the work they do and wants to be happy in the place they work.
   - Purpose has become increasingly important for some organizations to consider a C-suite-level director of purpose. A happy worker has become important enough that research has begun to show that a happy worker with a purpose is healthier, more intrinsically motivated, has higher job satisfaction, is less stressed, is more productive, and can lead to lower attrition and a more engaged workforce.

4. **<u>Diverse Team</u>**—A diverse team is all about the <u>diversity of the workforce</u>, as well as ensuring that all team members feel included and are given equal opportunities to contribute. Diversity has been described as **any dimension that can be used to differentiate groups and individuals from one another.**
   - **<u>Why might this be important</u>**? Diversity is about empowering people by respecting and appreciating what makes them different, in

terms of age, gender, ethnicity, religion, disability, sexual orientation, education, and national origin. When leaders and organizational culture support and leverage their diverse workforce, it leads to greater collaboration, which is important for diversity and effective team dynamics.

- An effective team has been defined as a group of people with complementary skills, committed to a common purpose, mutual goals, and a well-defined approach to work. Effective team members trust each other and hold themselves accountable.

5. **Safe**: This component is about <u>psychological safety</u>. Psychological safety in the workplace refers to the collective belief or recognition that any member of the organization can express their perspective and opinion (even if it is a minority point of view) without fear of punishment, exclusion, or humiliation.

   - **Why might this be important?** In a workplace that promotes psychological safety, employees are more likely to feel comfortable expressing their ideas and personalities, as there is a greater sense of trust and respect in the environment. In today's workplace, where innovation and creativity can provide a competitive advantage, psychological safety will be important. To have an organization where innovation and creativity are valued, you need an environment where risks and mistakes are accepted, and where workers feel safe.

6. **Listening**: This is about <u>communication and how</u> effective leaders are at communicating and listening to the concerns, ideas, and uniqueness of each of their team members. It's about how leaders listen, are empathetic, and compassionate when listening to their workers' issues and concerns.

   - **Why might this be important**? Listening leads to learning. Communication and listening are imperative to the success of leaders and their workforce. As busy as leaders are, when they listen to understand and not to respond, this leads to a more engaged workforce. When leaders are empathetic and compassionate, this is driven by effective listening and communication. Empathy has been defined as the ability to understand or feel what another person is experiencing from their frame of reference, that is, the ability to put themselves in the place of the other.

Leader Behavior Effectiveness (LBE) Questionnaire

Perception of My Leadership Behaviors: Self and Team Evaluation

The following is a questionnaire for you to complete and reflect on. It is intended to assist you on focusing on your development as you move into the new role or your current role of supervisor, manager, director, VP, CEO, in essence as "the boss." Complete it honestly and candidly. This is intended for you as a starting point, to reflect on your behaviors and as part of your ongoing development as a leader. This questionnaire is intended to have you reflect on your leadership behaviors and gain insight into what others observe and perceive. In essence, it is intended to help you help yourself. With this questionnaire you can consider partnering with an Executive Coach or continue on your own developmental journey as a leader as you look to always improve.

My Effectiveness as a Leader

The rating scale is:

1-Strongly Disagree (SD)	2-Disagree (D)	3-Neutral (N)
4-Agree (A)	5-Strongly Agree (SA)	Leave blank anything that does not apply

1. I believe I communicate my expectations, directions, and instructions clearly.

1	2	3	4	5
SD	D	N	A	SA

2. I believe I listen to concerns of my team and staff members.

1	2	3	4	5
SD	D	N	A	SA

3. I provide on-going feedback and share my appreciation for the work my team members do.

1	2	3	4	5

SD   D   N   A   SA

4. I am open to feedback on how I support my team members and provide a great workplace experience.

1	2	3	4	5
SD	D	N	A	SA

5. I am open to other ways of addressing an issue that someone might surface.

1	2	3	4	5
SD	D	N	A	SA

6. When an issue or problem arises, I engage as needed to enable my subordinates and team to achieve success.

1	2	3	4	5
SD	D	N	A	SA

7. I believe I am a strong team development leader.

1	2	3	4	5
SD	D	N	A	SA

8. I treat all of my subordinate's fair and do not demonstrate favoritism.

1	2	3	4	5
SD	D	N	A	SA

9. I create an excellent workplace experience and environment where everyone remains engaged in the work, they are involved in.

1	2	3	4	5
SD	D	N	A	SA

10. I work with each of my subordinates to develop their developmental opportunities and maximize their strengths.

1	2	3	4	5
SD	D	N	A	SA

11. I believe I create a trusting and psychologically safe work environment and work to create a transparent workplace.

1	2	3	4	5
SD	D	N	A	SA

12. I am sensitive to the diversity of our team members and see this as a strength for our team and department.

1	2	3	4	5
SD	D	N	A	SA

13. If individuals work away from my primary location, I make an extra effort to reach out and ensure they are engaged and that their needs are being met.

1	2	3	4	5
SD	D	N	A	SA

14. I communicate up to my management team, my team/department challenges, and successes.

1	2	3	4	5
SD	D	N	A	SA

15. I believe I am a good boss and demonstrate quality management and leadership skills.

1	2	3	4	5
SD	D	N	A	SA

Reflections, thoughts, takeaways, themes, action plan: What I believe I do well and what I could do better.

_____
_____
_____

Perception From Others on My Leadership Behaviors

The following is an evaluation for you to have your staff, colleagues, and superior complete on you. You can provide this directly to them and have them provide you their completed instrument or you can create a process whereby the feedback is anonymous.

It is intended for you to gain insights into what others think of your management and leadership behaviors. With this input along with your own completed assessment can serve as a powerful reflection tool and activity. It is intended to assist you on focusing on your development as you move into the new role of supervisor, manager, in essence as "the boss." The key here is not to be defensive on the feedback you get, but to ensure you understand what it is saying and develop a plan to work on it. This is intended for you as a starting point in your ongoing development as a someone in a leadership role.

After you complete your evaluation and get feedback from others you may want to partner with an Executive Coach, your HR Business Partner, or someone that can help you reflect and develop an action plan for yourself to continue to improve your effectiveness. You will also want to share with those that completed the instrument on you what you've learned and what you hope to work on moving forward.

Input on: _____

This input is from the perspective of (underline or circle one): staff, colleague, supervisor, other

The rating scale is:

Scale: 1-Strongly Disagree (SD), 2-Disagree (D), 3-Neutral (N), 4-Agree (A), 5-Strongly agree (SA)

1. I believe our leaders demonstrate effective leadership by creating a positive workplace experience.

1	2	3	4	5
SD	D	N	A	SA

2. I believe this individual listens to concerns of the team, staff members, and colleagues.

1	2	3	4	5
SD	D	N	A	SA

3. She/he provides on-going feedback and share their appreciation for the work the team members do.

1	2	3	4	5
SD	D	N	A	SA

4. He/she is open to feedback on how they support the team members and create a great workplace experience.

1	2	3	4	5
SD	D	N	A	SA

5. She/he is open to other ways of addressing an issue that someone might surface.

1	2	3	4	5
SD	D	N	A	SA

6. When an issue or problem arises, they engage as needed to enable the subordinates and team to achieve success.

1	2	3	4	5
SD	D	N	A	SA

7. I believe this individual is a strong team development supervisor.

1	2	3	4	5
SD	D	N	A	SA

8. He/she treat all of their subordinate's fair and do not demonstrate favoritism.

1	2	3	4	5
SD	D	N	A	SA

9. He/she creates an empowering environment where everyone remains engaged in the work, they are involved in.

1	2	3	4	5
SD	D	N	A	SA

10. She/he works with each of their subordinates to develop their developmental areas and maximize their strengths.

1	2	3	4	5
SD	D	N	A	SA

11. I believe this individual creates a trusting work environment and works to create a transparent workplace.

1	2	3	4	5
SD	D	N	A	SA

12. This individual is sensitive to the diversity of the team members and see this as a strength for the team and department.

1	2	3	4	5
SD	D	N	A	SA

13. If individuals work away from the primary location of this individual, they make the extra effort to reach out and ensure they are engaged and that their needs are being met.

1	2	3	4	5
SD	D	N	A	SA

14. This individual communicates up to their management team, the team/department challenges, and successes.

1	2	3	4	5
SD	D	N	A	SA

15. I believe this individual is a good boss and demonstrates quality management and leadership skills.

1	2	3	4	5
SD	D	N	A	SA

Demographics (Optional)

Gender:	Female___	Male___	No opinion___	
Age:	Below 30___	31–40___	41–50___	51 and older___
Tenure:	1 year or less___	1+ to 5 years___	5+ to 10 years___	10+ years___

Comments/What Do They Do Well/What They Could Do Better

_____
_____
_____
_____
_____
_____
_____

Key Considerations on the Feedback

Take a look at the themes and insights from the input from others and compare them to your insights/perceptions. Particularly, you should look for items in particular such as communications, leadership skills, etc. Pay particular attention where there might be a difference as to how you see yourself and how others see you.

REFERENCES

Accenture. (2022). Human connection and trust unlock productivity, retention and revenue growth. https://newsroom.accenture.com/news/human-connection-and-trust-unlock-productivity-retention-and-revenue-growth-accenture-research-finds.htm

Aguh, C., & Etzwilier, D. (2023). The people 2030 conference. https://www.conference-board.org/events/attendeePortal/talent-event

Aldrich, S. (2016). How good bosses increase productivity. https://www.linkedin.com/pulse/how-good-bosses-increase-productivity-steven-aldrich

Andalibi, N. (2024). Emotion-tracking AI is making some workers' challenges worse. https://www.fastcompany.com/91052850/emotion-tracking-ai-worker-challenges

Augustine, N. (2007). *Rising above the gathering storm: Energizing and employing America for a brighter economic future.* Committee on Prospering in the Global Economy of the 21st Century.

Bailey, J. (2016). The difference between good leaders and great ones. *HBR.* https://hbr.org/2016/09/the-difference-between-good-leaders-and-great-ones

Beer, M., Finnstrom, M., & Schrader, D. (2016). Why leadership training fails-and what to do about it. https://hbr.org/2016/10/why-leadership-training-fails-and-what-to-do-about-it

Berman, R. (2016). *How Deloitte build bridges in their organizational culture.* Bloomberg. http://www.bloomberg.com/features/2015-the-edge-the-worlds-greenest-building/

Bersin, J. (2016). The future of work: It's already here – And not as scary as you think. *Forbes.* http://www.forbes.com/sites/joshbersin/2016/09/21/the-future-of-work-its-already-here-and-not-as-scary-as-you-think/#433391a85506

Bersin, J. (2023). Microsoft work trends 2022 & Gallup global engagement. https://www.humanresourcesonline.net/the-workforce-in-2022-15-trends-that-will-shape-hiring-learning-working-and-more

Bersin, J., & Chomorro-Premuzic, T. (2019). The case for hiring older workers. *Harvard Business Review.* https://hbr.org/2019/09/the-case-for-hiring-older-workers

Boston Consulting Group (BCG). (2024). Getting ready for the jobs of the future. https://www.linkedin.com/pulse/getting-ready-jobs-future-boston-consulting-group-ti7nc/?midToken=AQGXy0vK26kp8g&midSig=17kpFi0IRjsHc1&trk=eml-email_series_follow_newsletter_01-newsletter_content_preview-0-headline_&trkEmail=eml-email_series_follow_newsletter_01-newsletter_content_preview-0-headline_-null-w5vx~lulegc6i~mz-null-null&eid=w5vx-lulegc6i-mz&otpToken=MTMwMDFlZTAxNDJjYzhjZWI1MjkwNGU4NDQxYWUyYjI4Y2M4ZDM0MTllYTQ4YjYyNzNjMzAzNmM0ZTUzNWZmOTk0ZDBiMzhiNGNNlMWMyZDdlYjM0OGY3MDY5NjU3NWFkN2NiNGNjNjNjNTlmYmI3NWWQ5MiwxLDE%3D

Bradberry, T. (2024). 7 things fabulous listeners do differently. https://www.linkedin.com/pulse/7-things-fabulous-listeners-do-differently-dr-travis-bradberry-lunye/?trackingId=9YZ5p%2B7f9mVVk98s4RKhag%3D%3D

Branham, L. (2012). *The 7 hidden reasons employees leave.* AMACOM Books.

Brighton, D. (2016). 10 reasons why culture matters. http://blog.mytalentlab.com/2016/10/10-reasons-why-culture-matters.html

Bryant, A. (2023). *The leap to leader.* https://hbr.org/2023/07/the-leap-to-leader

Burg, N. (2016). 5 factors that add up to employee happiness. *Fortune.* http://www.forbes.com/sites/adp/2016/10/10/5-factors-that-add-up-to-employee-happiness/#7f51667f32a0

Campbell, S. (2016, April). *The Millennials are coming* (p. 14). Association of Talent & Development (ATD) Magazine.

Cawood, S. (2023). *The new work exchange: Embracing the future by putting employees first.* Forbes Books.

Chamorro-Premuzic, T. (2020). Why do so many incompetent men become leaders? And what we can do about it. https://hbr.org/2013/08/why-do-so-many-incompetent-men

Chamorro-Premuzic, T., & Carucci, R. (2024). 85% of new people managers receive no formal training. This is why you can't fake it. https://www.fastcompany.com/91088693/85-of-new-people-managers-receive-no-formal-training-this-is-why-you-cant-fake-it

Cheng, R. (2016). Apple has 1 billion active devices around the world. http://www.cnet.com/news/apple-has-1-billion-active-devices-around-the-world/

Colvin, G. (2015). *Humans are underrated: What high achievers know that brilliant machines never will.* Portfolio/Penguin.

Congleton, C., Hotzel, B., & Lazar, S. (2019, January). *Mindfulness can literally change your brain.* Harvard Business. Review Special Issue.

Coughlin, J. (2017). *The longevity economy: Unlocking the world's fastest-growing, most misunderstood market.* Public Affairs.

Cuddy, A. (2012). Your body language may shape who you are. https://www.ted.com/talks/amy_cuddy_your_body_language_may_shape_who_you_are?language=en

Daly, L. (2023). *Remote work saves workers 72 minutes per day. Here's how to make the most of it.* https://www.fool.com/the-ascent/personal-finance/articles/remote-work-saves-workers-72-minutes-per-day-heres-how-to-make-the-most-of-it/#:~:text=By%20eliminating%20commutes%2C%20remote%20work%20saves%20people%2072,save%20for%20something%20productive%2C%20like%20errands%20or%20goals

Davis, K. (2024). 5 things all good bosses have in common. https://www.msn.com/en-us/money/careers/5-things-all-good-bosses-have-in-common/ar-BB1jHy4R?ocid=BingHp01&cvid=d34a031d8e0746e3c344798d978d4481&ei=14

Ding, Y., & Ma, M. (2023). Return to office mandates. https://papers.ssrn.com/sol3/papers.cfm?abstract_id=4675401

Donnelly, S. (2023). Managing complex change matrix for CFOs (Lippett-Knoster model). https://www.financealliance.io/managing-complex-change-matrix/

Drucker, P. (2002, February). *They're not employees, they're people*. Harvard Business Review.

Edmondson, A. (2018). *The fearless organization: Creating psychological safety in the workplace for learning, innovation, and growth*. Wiley.

Egan, M. (2024). 4-day workweeks may be around the corner. A third of America's companies are exploring them. https://www.cnn.com/2024/04/12/business/four-day-workweek-survey?cid=ios_app

Ellingrud, K., Sanghvi, S., Dandona, G., Madgavkar, A., Chui, M., White, O., & Hasebe, P. (2023). Generative AI and the future of work in America. https://www.mckinsey.com/mgi/our-research/generative-ai-and-the-future-of-work-in-america

Elliott, B. (2025). The great office divide. https://theworkforward.substack.com/p/the-great-office-divide

Elliott, B., Subramanian, S., & Kupp, H. (2022). *How the future works: Leading flexible teams to do the best work of their lives*. John Wiley & Sons, Inc.

Erickson, R., Kohler, L., King, G., & Roberts, M. (2023). Creating a more "Human-Centered" workplace to address service and manufacturing labor shortages. https://www.conference-board.org/topics/tags.cfm?parent=labor-shortages&child=Creating-More-Human-Centered-Workplace

Evian, G., Leanne, W., Megan, O., Nicholas, C., & Savannah, D. (2010). *Neuroleadership and the productive brain*. https://membership.neuroleadership.com/material/neuroleadership-and-the-productive-brain-vol-3/

Falzon, R. (2021). Analysis: There won't be a skills gap in jobs, "We're going to see a skills canyon". https://finance.yahoo.com/video/analyst-wont-skills-gap-jobs-204327240.html?guccounter=1&guce_referrer=aHR0cHM6Ly93d3cubGlua2VkaW4uY29tLw&guce_referrer_sig=AQAAANu7I4DjaQlmKBa1D_D4l7qRv-Ie2zA2uiSx7IUR5zIv5JlAYaX_3XBUNWri2aBcPK4hRG2bksoEDtyC4MwqRR8fqeIAKRfmR7bJtt8AypQJrVtSS7EQKc4N6-G0uXKgVATVmfO6KT-G4wQlHhwz7T8myeMlwkT3qDLx_DhlYnkPt

Ferrer, B. (2024). Leaders, here are 4 ways you're inadvertently destroying trust in the workplace (and what to do instead). https://www.msn.com/en-us/money/careers/leaders-here-are-4-ways-you-re-inadvertently-destroying-trust-in-the-workplace-and-what-to-do-instead/ar-BB1j3klX?ocid=BingHp01&cvid=3a74086eca1f497cea6f88c9ae1ffe8a&ei=20

Field, E., Hancock, B., & Schaninger, B. (2023). *Don't eliminate your middle managers*. Harvard Business Review. https://hbr.org/2023/07/dont-eliminate-your-middle-managers

Fisher, A. (2015). *American millennials among the world's least skilled*. Fortune.

Fleming, V. (Director). (1939). *The wizard of oz* [Film]. Metro-Goldwyn-Mayer.

Followan, K. (2023). The effect of remote work on firm level productivity. *Gettysburg Economic Review, 12*, 4. https://cupola.gettysburg.edu/ger/vol12/iss1/4

Frank, M., & Roehrig, P. (2014). *Code halos: How the digital lives of people, things, and organizations are changing the rules of business.* John Wiley & Sons, Inc.

Friedman, T. L. (2005). *The world is flat: A brief history of the twenty-first century.* Farrar, Straus and Giroux.

Gallup Consulting. (2008). Employee engagement: What's your engagement ratio? http://www.americasdiversityleader.com/Downloads/Employee_Engagement_Overview_Brochure.pdf

Gallup Consulting. (2024a). Managers who have better conversations have stronger teams. https://www.linkedin.com/feed/Managers who have better conversations have better teams

Gallup Consulting. (2024b). State of the global workplace: The voice of the world's employees. https://www.gallup.com/workplace/349484/state-of-the-global-workplace.aspx#ite-645944

Gartner. (2023). Managers are cracking and more training won't help. https://emtemp.gcom.cloud/ngw/globalassets/en/human-resources/documents/managers-are-cracking-and-more-training-wont-help.pdf

Gentry, W., Eckert, R., Stawski, S., & Zhao, S. (2015). The challenges leaders face around the world: More similar than different. http://insights.ccl.org/wp-content/uploads/2015/04/ChallengesLeadersFace.pdf

Gilson, L., Maynard, M. T., Young, N. C., Vartiainen, M., & Hakonen, M. (2015). Virtual teams research: 10 years, 10 themes, and 10 opportunities. *Journal of Management, 41*(5), 1313–1337.

Glaser, J., & Glaser, R. (2019, January). *The neurochemistry of positive conversations.* Harvard Business Review.

Goleman, D., & Boyatzis, R. (2019, January). *Social intelligence and the biology of leadership.* Harvard Business Review.

Good, L. (2016). Are you prepared for a shifting workforce? https://www.linkedin.com/pulse/you-prepared-shifting-workforce-lynn-good?trk=hp-feed-article-title-share

Gordon, E. (2013). *The global talent crisis: Contrary to popular opinion, there are plenty of open jobs. What's missing are candidates with skills.* https://commons.wvc.edu/jminharo/pols206/Article%20to%20Choose%20From/Global%20Talent.pdf

Green, D. (2024). The best HR & people analytics articles of 2023 (Part 1 of 2). https://www.linkedin.com/pulse/best-hr-people-analytics-articles-2023-part-1-2-david-green-qv42e%3FtrackingId=pM%252BByLTwBNxybR451YhgDQ%253D%253D/?trackingId=pM%2BByLTwBNxybR451YhgDQ%3D%3D

Hamel, G., & Zanini, M. (2020). *Humanocracy: Creating organizations as amazing as the people inside them.* Harvard Business Review Press.

Hart, L. (2016). Building trust in the workplace. http://www.journalofaccountancy.com/newsletters/2016/sep/building-trust-in-workplace.html

Hill, L. (2007, January). *Becoming the boss.* Harvard Business Review.

Ho, B. (2021). *Why trust matters: An economist's guide to the ties that bind us.* Columbia Press.

Hogan. (2016). 4 ways to build trust. http://info.hoganassessments.com/4-ways-to-build-trust

Hollins, P. (2019). *Build a better brain: Using neuroplasticity to train your brain for motivation, discipline, courage, and mental sharpness.* Independently Published.

Hougaard, R., Carter, J., & Sorenson, A. (2018). *The mind of the leader: How to lead yourself, your people, and your organization for extraordinary results*. Harvard Business Press Review.

Hougaard, R., Carter, J., & Stembridge, R. (2024). The best leaders can't be replaced by AI. https://hbr.org/2024/01/the-best-leaders-cant-be-replaced-by-ai

Howard-Grenville, J. & Empson, L. (2023, September 28). *3 ways to prepare for the future of work*. Harvard Business Review.

HP Research. (2023). First HP work relationship index shows majority of people worldwide have an unhealthy relationship with work. https://press.hp.com/us/en/press-releases/2023/hp-work-relationship-index.html

Huber, E. (2023). I don't want to manage. https://www.predictiveindex.com/blog/i-dont-want-to-manage-people/?utm_source=linkedin&utm_medium=website&utm_campaign=social

IBM Study. (2022). Building human-centered organizations. https://www.ibm.com/design/thinking/page/hco#introduction

Insperity Staff. (2023). Mastering leadership: 10 must-have traits of great bosses. https://www.insperity.com/blog/traits-of-great-bosses/

Jackson, A. (2023a). 3 soft skills separate highly successful CEOs from most people – Here's how to master them. https://www.cnbc.com/2023/05/03/these-soft-skills-separate-highly-successful-ceos-from-most-people.html

Jackson, A. (2023b). Bosses with these 3 toxic habits have low emotional intelligence. *Harvard-trained psychologist says*. https://www.msn.com/en-us/health/other/bosses-with-these-3-toxic-habits-have-low-emotional-intelligence-harvard-trained-psychologist-says/ar-AA1mSFdr?ocid=BingHp01&cvid=316dc9d0923d43f9dc485657ec42af5f&ei=14

Johansen, B., Press, J., & Bullen, C. (2023). *Office shock: Creating better futures for working and living*. Berrett-Koehler Publishers, Inc.

Kissinger, H., Schmidt, E., & Huttenlocher, D. (2021). *The age of AI and our human future*. Little, Brown and Company.

Klemm, W. (2016). The perils of multitasking: Your smart phone can make you dumb. https://www.psychologytoday.com/us/blog/memory-medic/201608/the-perils-multitasking

Knotts, J. (2023). Seven ways to become a human-centered business. https://www.forbes.com/sites/forbescoachescouncil/2023/06/12/seven-ways-to-become-a-human-centered-business/?sh=75620a145e74

Kotter, J. (2007). *Leading change: Why transformation efforts fail*. Harvard Business Review.

Kraaijenbrink, J. (2022). What BANI really means (and how it corrects your world view). *Forbes*. https://www.forbes.com/sites/jeroenkraaijenbrink/2022/06/22/what-bani-really-means-and-how-it-corrects-your-world-view/?sh=3ee88b411bb3

Krogstad, J., Lopez, M., Lopez, G., Passel, J., & Patten, E. (2016). *Millennials make up almost half of the latino eligible voters in 2016*. PEW Research. http://www.pewhispanic.org/2016/01/19/millennials-make-up-almost-half-of-latino-eligible-voters-in-2016/

Kulp, P. (2024). Accenture's chief AI officer thinks every C-suite needs a job like hers. https://www.emergingtechbrew.com/stories/2024/04/04/chief-ai-officer-accenture-lan-guan

Le Cren, M. (2016). How to build a culture of collaboration. http://blog.azendoo. com/build-culture-of-collaboration/

Lee, S. (2056). Radical candor—The surprising secret to being a good boss. *LinkedIn.* https://www.linkedin.com/pulse/radical-candor-surprising-secret-being-good-boss-suzanna-lee

LinkedIn Learning. (2024). Closing the talent gap: To keep pace with innovation, organizations must help software engineers and IT pros build both hard and soft skills. https://learning.linkedin.com/resources/learning-insights/closing-the-tech-talent-gap?trk=bl-po&veh=Elevate_Your_Tech_Team

Llopis, G. (2015). *Without Hispanics Americas corporations can't grow and compete.* Forbes.

Lofranco, F. (2021). Five superpowers every manager needs: How navigating human relationships is the key to managerial success. https://irc.queensu.ca/five-superpowers-every-manager-needs/

Lombardo, B., & Meyerson, R. (2024). *Baby boomers still striving.* The Conference Board.

Lucas, E. (2023). The fastest growing demographic in the workforce? People over age 75. https://www.forbes.com/sites/emmylucas/2023/12/14/the-fastest-growing-demographic-in-the-workforce-people-over-age-75/?sh=1ddc621a1fcf

Lynn, B., & Sarro, E. (2022). Five things you may not know about psychological safety. https://neuroleadership.com/your-brain-at-work/5-things-psych-safety

Mackey, J., & Sisodia, R. (2013). *Conscious capitalism: Liberating the heroic spirit of business.* Harvard Business School Publishing Corp.

Maitland, A., & Thomson, P. (2011). *Future work: How business can adapt and thrive in the new world of work.* Palgrave Macmillan.

Maurer, R. (2010). *Beyond the wall of resistance.* Bard Press.

Medina, J. (2008). *Brain rules: 12 principles for surviving and thriving at work, school, and home.* Pear Press.

Medina, J. (2014). *Brain rules: 12 principles for surviving and thriving at work.* Pear Press.

Medina, J. (2017). *Brain rules for aging well: 10 principles for staying vital, happy, and sharp.* Pear Press.

Medina, J. (2021). *Brain rules for work: The science of thinking smarter in the office and at home.* Goodreads Press.

Merisotis, J. (2020). *Human work in the age of smart machines.* Rosetta Books.

Miami Herald. (2017). Best bosses we ever had inspired, challenged and cared, say South Florida CEOs. http://www.miamiherald.com/news/business/bizmonday/article157525714.html

Michelman, P. (2016, Fall). *Management's digital future has arrived* (Vol. 58). MIT Sloan Management Review.

Minks, C. (2024). The future of your brain. *Superpower-Breaking bad habits.*

Mintzberg, H. (1975). *The manager's job: Folklore and fact.* Harvard Business Review.

Morgan, J. (2017). *The employee experience advantage: How to win the war for talent by giving employees the workspaces, they want, the tools the need, and the culture the can celebrate.* Wiley & Sons.

Morgan, K. (2021). Why in-person workers may be more likely to get promoted. https://www.bbc.com/worklife/article/20210305-why-in-person-workers-may-be-more-likely-to-get-promoted

Morgan, J. (2024). What everyone gets wrong about leadership, it's about you. https://www.youtube.com/watch?v=Iq3RYEBMDrY

Mosley, E., & Irvine, D. (2021). *Making work human: How human-centered companies are changing the future of work and the world.* McGraw-Hill.

Mouriño, E. (2014). *The perfect human capital storm: Workplace challenges & opportunities in the 21st century.* Create Space Publishing.

Nip, A. (2016). Lessons I've learnt as a manager. *LinkedIn.* https://www.linkedin.com/pulse/lessons-ive-learnt-manager-andrew-nip?trk=hp-feed-article-title-like

Partaker, E. (2024). Master these 8 soft skills to accelerate your career. https://www.linkedin.com/feed/

Perrin, C. (2010). Leader vs. manager: What's the distinction? http://www.rpi.edu/dept/hr/docs/Leadervsmanager.pdf

Pfeffer, J. (2015). *Leadership BS: Fixing workplaces and careers one truth at a time.* Harper/Collins.

Pfeffer, J. (2018). *Dying for a paycheck: How modern management harms employee health and company performance-and what we can do about it.* Harper/Collins.

Pickup, O. (2022). Why bosses are struggling more than ever. https://www.worklife.news/leadership/under-pressure-why-bosses-are-struggling-more-than-ever/?utm_campaign=worklifedis&utm_source=worklifedaily&utm_medium=email&utm_content=71123&utm_medium=email&utm_campaign=Worklife%20Briefing%2007112023&utm_content=Worklife%20Briefing%2007112023+CID_ba3ab70302cc5294817d09edae1cdc45&utm_source=wldis&utm_term=Under%20pressure%20Why%20bosses%20are%20struggling%20more%20than%20ever

Pink, D. (2009). The puzzle of motivation. https://www4.bing.com/videos/search?q=dan+pink+motivation&view=detail&mid=3D64C9F59CBA08DCBD6F3D64C9F59CBA08DCBD6F&FORM=VIRE

Platt, M. (2020). *The leader's brain: Enhance your leadership, build stronger teams, make better decisions, and inspire greater innovation with neuroscience.* Wharton School Press.

Posner, E., & Whitehouse, T. (2023). Learning and development for the workforce of the future. https://deloitte.wsj.com/cio/learning-and-development-for-the-workforce-of-the-future-2beb092d

Reed, B. (2024). AI will affect 40% of jobs and probably worsen inequality, says IMF head. https://www.theguardian.com/technology/2024/jan/15/ai-jobs-inequality-imf-kristalina-georgieva

Rock, D. (2013). Why organizations fail. *Fortune Magazine.* https://fortune.com/2013/10/23/why-organizations-fail/

Rock, D., & Ringleb, A. H. (2013). *Handbook of neuroleadership.* CreateSpace Independent Publishing Platform.

Rodriguez, R. (2008). *Latino talent: Effective strategies to recruit, retain and develop Hispanic professionals.* John Wiley & Sons, Inc.

Royal, M., & Stark, M. (2016). How the world's most admired companies are preparing for the future. *Fortune.* http://fortune.com/2016/02/19/worlds-most-admired-companies-preparing-future/

Sahadi, J. (2024). Hispanic and Latino professionals feel overlooked and under-represented in corporate America, new study finds. https://www.cnn.com/2024/04/10/success/hispanic-latino-professionals-feel-overlooked-stereotyped/index.html

Samples, M. (2024). 90% of leaders fail. They hide their emotions. https://www.linkedin.com/feed/update/urn:li:activity:7184158333904257024/

Schein, E. (1992). *Organizational culture and leadership* (2nd ed.). Jossey-Bass.

Schwab, K. (2018). *Shaping the 4th industrial revolution*. World Economic Forum.

Schwantes, M. (2024a). Google research says what separates the best managers from the rest boils down to 8 traits. https://www.msn.com/en-us/money/other/google-research-says-what-separates-the-best-managers-from-the-rest-boils-down-to-8-traits/ar-BB1ipOHd?ocid=BingHp01&cvid=b7f820d3f7534f46e4c120a9623db94b&ei=13

Schwantes, M. (2024b). 5 signs you're a better leader than you think. https://www.linkedin.com/pulse/5-signs-youre-better-leader-than-you-think-marcel-schwantes-tlhye/

Schwartz, J., & Riss, S. (2021). *Work disrupted: Opportunity, resilience, and growth in the accelerated future of work*. John Wiley & Sons.

Seppala, E., & Cameron, K. (2015). *Proof that positive work cultures are more productive*. Harvard Business Review. https://hbr.org/2015/12/proof-that-positive-work-cultures-are-more-productive

Siner, E., Wellins, R., & Paese, M. (2016). What's the number 1 leadership skill for overall success? http://www.ddiworld.com/global-offices/united-states/press-room/what-is-the-1-leadership-skill-for-overall-success

Smith, A., & Green, M. (2018). Artificial intelligence and the role of the leader. *The Journal of Leadership Studies, 12*(3). https://onlinelibrary.wiley.com/doi/abs/10.1002/jls.21605

Spisak, B. (2023). *Computational leadership: Connecting behavioral science and technology to optimize decision-making and increase profits*. Wiley.

Strack, R. (2014). The workforce crisis of 2030 and how to start solving it now. http://www.ted.com/talks/rainer_strack

Swain, B. (2016). *Successful leaders know what made them who they are*. Harvard Business Review (HBR). https://hbr.org/2016/09/successful-leaders-know-what-made-them-who-they-are

Swart, T., Chisholm, K., & Brown, P. (2015). *Neuroscience for leadership: Harnessing the brain gain advantage*. White Paper. Truist Leadership Institute.

Swavely, S. (2020). Your brain on purpose: The neuropsychology of leadership purpose. https://www.truistleadershipinstitute.com/content/dam/truistleadershipinstitute/us/en/documents/whitepaper/neuropsychology-of-leadership-purpose.pdf

Swavely, S. (2023). *Ignite your leadership: The power of neuropsychology to optimize team performance*. Indie Books.

Swavely, S. (2024a). The power of human connection in a digital age. https://evolutionleadershipcoaching.com/blog/f/the-power-of-human-connection-in-a-digital-age

Swavely, S. (2024b). Unlocking leadership brilliance: The neuropsychology behind inspirational leaders. https://www.linkedin.com/pulse/unlocking-leadership-brilliance-neuropsychology-swavely-ph-d-ccp-uex7e%3FtrackingId=zIzO3UZw1MKIWzXD67ihFw%253D%253D/?trackingId=zIzO3UZw1MKIWzXD-67ihFw%3D%3D

Tamayo, J., Doumi, L., Goel, S., Kovacs-Ondrejkovic, O., & Sadun, R. (2023, September-October). *Reskilling in the age of AI.* Harvard Business Review.

Tara, S., Chilshom, K., & Brown, P. (2015). *Neuroscience for leadership: Harnessing the brain gain advantage.* Palgrave MacMillan.

Taylor, J. C. Jr (2021). *Reset: A leader's guide to work in an age of upheaval.* Hatchett Book Groups, LLC.

Taylor, J. C. Jr (2024). Top 10 skills that will rise in importance in the next 5 years. https://www.linkedin.com/posts/johnnyctaylorjr_shrm-hr-skillsgap-activity-7186020294694723586-Ldi2/?utm_source=share&utm_medium=member_ios

Thacker, J. W. (2013). *Effective training: Systems, strategies, and practices* (5th ed.). Pearson.

The Conference Board. (2022). Harnessing the power of the multi-generational workforce. https://www.conference-board.org/webcast/ondemand/2022-September

The future of jobs report 2023. *World Economic Forum.* https://www.weforum.org/reports/the-future-of-jobs-report-2023/digest

Van Quaquebeke, N., & Gerpott, F. H. (2023). The now, new, and next digital leadership: How artificial intelligence (AI) will take over and change leadership as we know it. *Journal of Leadership & Organizational Studies.* https://journals.sagepub.com/doi/full/10.1177/15480518231181731

Volini, E., Schwartz, J., Eaton, K., & Mallon, D. (2021). The social enterprise in a world disrupted: Leading the shift form survive to thrive. *2021 Deloitte Global HumanCapital Trends.* https://www2.deloitte.com/ua/en/pages/about-deloitte/press-releases/gx-2021-global-human-capital-trends-report.html

Westover, J. H. (2025). *The human-centered workplace: Cultivating meaning, motivation, and transformative leadership.* HCI Academic Press.

Watkins, M. (2003). *The first 90 days.* Harvard Business School Publishing.

Watz, A., & Mason, M. (2019, January). *Your brain at work.* Harvard Business Review.

Wayas, I. (2023). AI fallacy: Why comparing human intelligence to AI could be a mistake for white-collar workers. https://www.msn.com/en-us/news/technology/ai-fallacy-why-comparing-human-intelligence-to-ai-could-be-a-mistake-for-white-collar-workers/ar%20AA1jFqu4?ocid=BingHp01&cvid=acb8fbf8160c465ac078d5eb145bc31e&ei=21

Whitter, B. (2019). *Employee experience: Develop a happy, productive and supported workforce for exceptional individual and business performance.* Kogan Page Limited.

Wigert, B. (2023). 6 workplace trends leaders should watch in 2024. *Gallup.* https://www.gallup.com/workplace/547283/workplace-trends-leaders-watch-2024.aspx?version=print

Wilner Golden, S. (2022). *Stage (not age): How to understand and serve people over 60 – the fastest growing, most dynamic market in the world.* Harvard Business School Publishing Corporation.

Winkle-Giulioni, J. (2024). Using artificial intelligence to deepen human intelligence. https://www.linkedin.com/pulse/using-artificial-intelligence-deepen-human-julie-winkle-giulioni-coa2c/

Wolper, J. (2016, April). *The need to upskill* (p. 18). Association for Talent & Development (ATD) magazine.

Wong, R. (2023). Young workers don't want to become managers – And this study uncovers the reason why. https://www.entrepreneur.com/leadership/young-workers-dont-want-to-become-managers-and-this/462273

Work Trend Index Special Report. (2021). Research proves your brain needs breaks. https://www.microsoft.com/en-us/worklab/work-trend-index/brain-research/

Yeo, C. (2020). Why organizations need human-centered leaders, and three tips to get started. *Forbes.* https://www.forbes.com/sites/forbescoachescouncil/2020/05/08/why-organizations-need-human-centered-leaders-and-three-tips-to-get-started/?sh=473f937b72ac

Yi, R. (2023). 6 worrying workplace numbers – And what you can do about them. *Gallup.* https://www.gallup.com/workplace/513491/worrying-workplace-numbers.aspx?version=print

Yildirim, E. (2023). Wharton psychologist on the 3 biggest challenges facing workers right now: 'We have a responsibility' to make them better. https://www.msn.com/en-us/money/careers/wharton-psychologist-on-the-3-biggest-challenges-facing-workers-right-now-we-have-a-responsibility-to-make-them-better/ar-AA1jZbfO?ocid=BingHp01&cvid=320a81af176542bcbd7f782977eb883f&ei=19

Young Entrepreneur Council (YEC). (2024). The best manager traits: 13 essential for great leadership. https://www.msn.com/en-us/money/smallbusiness/the-best-manager-traits-13-essentials-for-great-leadership/ar-AA1mM4zV?ocid=BingHp01&cvid=36730d60029d4757dea6db06d9799b62&ei=97

Zak, P. (2019, January). *The neuroscience of trust.* Harvard Business Review.

Zenger, J., & Folkman, J. (2019). The 3 elements of trust. https://hbr.org/2019/02/the-3-elements-of-%20trust?tpcc=orgsocial_edit&utm_campaign=hbr&utm_medium=social&utm_source=linkedin

www.ingramcontent.com/pod-product-compliance
Lightning Source LLC
Chambersburg PA
CBHW060320220326
41598CB00027B/4380